Carrying a Flag
From Pain to Passion

ANDREW BUERGER

Thanks for
your support of
JFS.

3/13/2023

keep climbing.
Andy

For Peter, Chaz, Caroline, and Max, whose
painful loss inspires me to find a cure.

For Jennifer, Joss, and Bronsten: thanks for keeping me grounded
while I climb higher and for giving me a great reason to come home.

In memory of Chuck, Brona, and Jodi. You will never be forgotten.

TABLE OF CONTENTS

CARRY A FLAG

"The two most important days in your life are the day
you are born and the day you find out why."

—Mark Twain

On November 7, 1996, I was working at my office. Jodi called me. My sister was living in Boston and was three weeks from having her first baby, the first baby in our generation.

My father was undergoing a procedure to replace his aortic valve, an operation performed on 182,000 Americans a year. He was at The Johns Hopkins Hospital in Baltimore, where he had bypass surgery a dozen years before.

Jodi relayed the information from the hospital that the surgery was taking longer than expected. The doctors were having some challenges getting to the heart because of the scar tissue from the previous bypass.

Only six weeks away from the official start of winter, Vancouver had gotten dark pretty early, around 4:30 p.m. I stayed at the office for a bit working and waiting for phone calls. Another call came at six o'clock from my other sister, Danielle. She's an alarmist, so I took her concern lightly. She tried relaying information from my cousin Meredith, who was an ER nurse. I felt like I was playing a game of phone tag from three time zones away. An eerie feeling crept into my gut. I wanted to leave the office. I had a new gadget on me called a cell phone that I could use to check in, no matter where I was.

Now pitch dark out, a cold drizzle started. I hopped in my Ford Explorer where the Wallflowers' song "6th Avenue Heartache" came on the radio. I drove past the harbor and industrial buildings making my life seem like a depressing scene in the Pacific Northwest-filmed movie *When Harry Met Sally.*

I called Jodi on my cell phone. She was worried. I drove to my girl-friend Amanda's retail store. I needed a hug and a landline. After sharing my fear with Amanda, I called my dad's good friend, Jan Guben. He had been one of the dozen people at the hospital that day. He gave it to me straight: the surgery didn't go well. The surgeon had a great deal of trouble getting to the heart through all the scar tissue from the last surgery. The surgeons kept him on a heart/lung machine for a long time, which thinned his blood. They nicked an artery that had been calcified from years of smoking and poor diet. It shattered. He lost a lot of blood, about half the blood in his body.

Jan told me that we had a tough road ahead. If my father lived he would likely be severely disabled. If he lived.

I went home and called my brother, who was also on the West Coast, living in L.A. "Kevin, you need to come home." I told him, "and pack a dark suit."

The next task was getting Jodi home. The doctors had her on bed rest for the home stretch of her pregnancy. She was sensible yet excitable. I was worried about getting her too emotional over Dad's situation so close to giving birth, and she wasn't supposed to fly. We decided to work with her cool and steady husband, Peter, to get Jodi home. Wrong decision. Peter was not particularly close to his father and was very close to mine. He was an emotional wreck. Jodi took care of the details and went to sleep.

Updates were not coming anymore, as all my family on the East Coast went to sleep. I booked a ticket on the first flight out the next morning, leaving at six. I finally got into bed just after midnight. I had a few hours to get some rest. It didn't matter that I had to get up at four o'clock. I knew I wouldn't be able to sleep much anyway. I lay awake. In my head I had a strange visualization that I was falling, falling, falling. I wasn't in any pain, because I was simply falling through the air. I would eventually have to hit the ground. I wasn't afraid of falling. It was hitting the ground eventually that I feared. I knew it was going to hurt.

My father was still alive, but I could feel it. I sensed it. I knew I had to leave Vancouver and get to Johns Hopkins Hospital. I wasn't convinced he'd recover from the surgery. My father was going to die. I was aware and stoic, focused on getting to see him. I knew when the realization hit that if I never saw him again, that's when the pain would be excruciating. I would hit the ground hard.

I set my alarm, but I didn't need it. I don't think I fell fully asleep, and I was wide awake just before four. I threw on some clothes, and Amanda took me to the airport. As we drove the dark, empty streets, I made Amanda stop to buy some fresh cinnamon rolls for my mom. She was going to need something to cheer her up.

I boarded the Northwest Airlines plane where I was able to cash in miles for some consolation to be seated in first class. The overly friendly steward drove me nuts. I wanted to be left alone. I had four hours until I had my layover in Minneapolis and the next update. A lot was going through my mind. I hated the unknown. I'd always been an optimist. I held out hope that there was a chance my father would pull through. Patience, though, wasn't my strength.

I couldn't wait to land at the Minneapolis airport for news about my father in the hospital. It was tearing me up. Was he alive? Was he going to be brain dead after losing so much blood during the operation? Was he going to be a vegetable?

It would be a few more hours before I could use the payphone in Minneapolis. Even though it was going to cost a fortune, I used the phone in the first-class cabin. I called the hospital room number my mother had given me. No one answered. Strange. Someone had to be there. I tried a few more times with no luck. Next, I called my home answering machine to see if anyone had left me a message. There was one message on the machine. It was from Peta Karabus, with whom I had recently become friendly since I moved to Vancouver eighteen months before.

The message came across in her thick South African accent. "Hi Andy, it's Peta. I'm so sorry to hear that your father died."

Chuck Buerger, the Best Ever

My father, Charles Alter Buerger, or Chuck, as the world knew him, lived a life with high peaks, like Everest, and low, low valleys, like Death Valley, and that made all the difference. If we were at sea level, he thought life was grand. Everything he experienced at sea level was "best ever, wonderful." He appreciated each moment that he wasn't in a trough. He wasn't always on a peak, but it didn't matter; he appreciated every moment of it.

My father's life story became my guidebook. I still remember where I was when my friend Daphne McCabe asked me a question. We were in a Boulder coffee shop when coffee shops were just starting to emerge in 1992. "Would you rather live life on an even keel with no major swings or a life that's full of large ups and downs?" she asked.

I didn't hesitate. "Peaks and valleys. Definitely."

One time I climbed Mount Whitney, the highest point in the lower forty-eight states at 14,500 feet. It was even more special that we drove through Death Valley, the lowest point in the U.S., experiencing both high and low in forty-eight hours.

Chuck Buerger was born on October 23, 1938, in Pittsburgh, Pennsylvania. The marriage of his parents, Geraldine and David, didn't last long. When Chuck was five, David walked out on Geraldine. Later we learned it was for another woman, but that's all for another book. For months Chuck waited by the window every night for his father to come home. He never did. Periodically David would call to see his son, but my father's pride and stubbornness seemed to have started at an early age. He refused to see his father, so David gave up on the young boy, and never called again. Chuck never had a father to play catch with him, which he lamented all his life.

Geraldine raised Chuck and his older sister, Susan, as a single working mother. We never knew if it was the stress or some sort of disease, but Geraldine had a number of maladies. Her eyesight deteriorated with retinitis pigmentosa-like symptoms. Her hearing also deteriorated to a large degree. In her mid-fifties, she was a very frail woman. She developed breast cancer that spread to her stomach, creating a prolonged, painful experience until she died in 1972 at age fifty-eight. Chuck was only thirty-two years old.

Up to his mother's death, my father remained very close to her, choosing to stay in Pittsburgh for college at what was then known as Carnegie Tech, now known as Carnegie Mellon University. It was just a few blocks from their house. He studied printing management. In his third year there he met Brona Sue Stein. Chuck graduated in 1960 and was drafted into the army where he served at Fort Rucker in Alabama. I heard that my father, while on weekend leave, drove twenty-four hours to visit Brona in Pittsburgh, spent a day, and then drove twenty-four hours back home.

Brona, born in the Mount Lebanon area of Pittsburgh, graduated from Carnegie Tech in 1962 and a month later, on June 20, married Chuck. After a brief honeymoon in Banff, they lived at Fort Rucker and eventually moved to Englewood, New Jersey, where Chuck sold printing. Kids followed quickly. Jodi was born eighteen months after their wedding, and I followed thirteen

Chuck & Brona

months after that. The young couple enjoyed spending time with neighbors and traveling in the Northeast.

Four years after their marriage they went "sailing" in Cape Cod for a week. By sailing I mean my father in a dinghy with a small mast and getting lost for hours. During that July trip, Brona seemed to develop a cold. A few weeks later, my mother got very sick to the point that she turned blue and couldn't speak. Dad rushed her to Englewood Hospital. The doctors couldn't do anything for her there, so she was transported to Sinai in New York City. She was diagnosed with thrombocytopenia purpura. It's a rare blood disease in which one's white blood cells attack the red blood cells. It's often fatal. The hospital performed a blood transfusion and removed her spleen. Two weeks later, on August 1, 1966, she died. She was twenty-five.

Chuck, a widower at twenty-seven years old and with a two-year girl, Jodi, and me, only a year old, was devastated. The love of his life was gone so quickly. He was a zombie for six months, barely able to function. Friends slept on the couch to pitch in. Relatives helped care for my sister and me. Neighbors had the tough job of removing Brona's clothes from the house and helping my father.

My father, ever the survivor, snapped out of it. He had to take care of his kids and provide for his family. He started to go out again. By February 1967 he met a woman at a party—Ronnie Uslan. They married seven months later. Ronnie adopted Jodi and me. They had three more children: Kevin, Danielle, and Lauren.

It's probably written in my DNA, and I watched it first-hand, so resiliency is both nature and nurture for me, giving me an extra dose.

My father dealt with challenges all his life. Each time, he kept moving forward, making the best of the situation and never complaining about it. Never. Everything was "wonderful." "Terrific." "Best ever." As a kid, his attitude drove me crazy. I loved the man dearly, and like all parents, they get on your nerves. He had an annoying habit of calling everything "The best ever." Every dinner out together. Every ski vacation. Every ski run. It became annoying, and then it became our running joke.

When I was very young, he told me a story.

Just after Brona died my father rode the elevator up to his office in New York City. This was at the time when men were actually operating them. Emotionally destroyed and stressed out about working and caring for two babies, he still made time to talk to the man running the elevator. The guy basically pushed the buttons.

"How's your day?" my father asked.

"Terrible," the man replied. "There's a couple moving out on the twelfth floor. Someone's moving in on the fourth. Other people have been needing the elevator. It's a very stressful day."

That, my father told me, shows that everyone's pain is relative. I never forgot that lesson.

My dad was the best father in the world, partly because he was making up for never having one, but he was the worst athlete and skier. The man skied for thirty years and could never get beyond a stem-christie turn. He took lessons every single year. I never understood that. I was a better and faster skier than him by the time I was ten, yet the man loved, loved, loved the sport. He knew that I had all my life to work a real job and saw my sister struggle living in a miserable place at age twenty-two. My dad "mandated" that I become a ski instructor, and that's made all the difference.

Dad became a legend in the newspaper publishing industry, running the family business started by my great-grandfather, David Alter, in 1919. Alter Communications published what was widely considered the best Jewish weekly newspaper in North America, the *Baltimore Jewish Times*.

My father expanded his business into several magazines and acquired or started Jewish publications in four more cities. With the larger operation, he decided to centralize the circulation marketing function. I had worked in Boulder for the largest subscription marketing firm in the country, so my father offered me the job to manage circulation for him. I left Boulder for Detroit. I sold my sunglasses and mountain bike, and my dream of hiking more of Colorado's 14,000-foot peaks—aka 14ers—sat on a shelf with my other outdoor equipment.

I worked in Detroit for two years, and it wasn't my thing. I needed mountains. The best thing that happened in Detroit was when my father told me he was investing in a publication in Vancouver, British Columbia, and needed me to move there.

I became the publisher of the Vancouver *Jewish Bulletin*, a little fixer-upper, and I loved every minute of it. I loved reinventing things. I wanted to prove myself, so I worked really hard. I was in the office early in the morning and left late. I'd even work six days a week.

The Kitsilano community in Vancouver was warm and welcoming, and a perfect location: four blocks north the beach, four blocks east of killer mountain-bike trails, and four blocks west of downtown that had cosmopolitan restaurants, bars, and coffee shops. On Fridays after a full day of work, we would drive up to what was considered the best ski resort in North America, Whistler/Blackcomb. It was only ninety minutes away. We'd party Friday, ski our tails off Saturday, party hard again Saturday night, and I'd be back at my desk by ten a.m. Sunday.

After my father died, our family huddled in the living room. I got the call from the bullpen. They wanted me to run the entire publishing operation. I was thirty-one years old.

There was a comedian in the 1980s named Steven Wright. He told the story of when his first child was born and he was in the delivery room. The doctor asked him to cut the umbilical cord, and he looked at the doctor and whined, "Isn't there someone a little more qualified?"

I reluctantly took the job and moved to Baltimore. I struggled dearly for the first several months. Not only was my best friend gone, but also I was unhappy away from the mountains. In the prior ten years, I'd lived in Vermont, Aspen, Boulder, and British Columbia. I had a bad case of altitude sickness—I was sick of not being at a higher altitude. For medicine, I climbed a few peaks and also visited the local Earth Treks climbing gym.

Slowly things got better for me. Even though I had to leave Vancouver, my girlfriend, and the Pacific Northwest outdoor life, I managed to escape back to the mountains often to help deal with everything. I also traveled the world both for fun and as the publisher of the Baltimore *Jewish Times*. I covered the Israeli war with Lebanon for work and trekked in Patagonia with my graduate school friends. I took climbing trips and business retreats to great places.

"Andy, it's cancer."

By 2004 my life was back in full swing. I had the new job thing figured out, our team at work had pulled out of a nosedive, and I was loving it. I had a friend, Deb, who was divorced with two boys and undergoing breast cancer treatment. I was helping her out, and despite her being bald, we fell in love and started a serious relationship. Everything was going my way.

I started to appreciate Baltimore, especially my Ravens, who won the Super Bowl in 2001. Our family had season tickets.

There was a Monday night game on October 4 against the Kansas City Chiefs. It was a gorgeous evening, and I spent time at the game with friends. KC held on despite a late Raven's touchdown. Even with the Ravens losing 27-24, dropping their record to 2-2, it was hard not to soak in the energy of the crowded downtown.

My father's friend Jan Guben gave me a ride to my car. Just before I opened the door to get out of Jan's car, my cell phone rang. I feel it's rude to talk on the phone in someone else's car, but I needed to take the call. I was waiting for the call. My sister, Jodi, had a meeting with her oncologist about her test results.

Jodi discovered a lump in her breast a week before that and went back to the doctor to see what it was. Now, I never see the glass as half-full; I see it all the way filled; overflowing in fact. I knew Jodi's test results would be negative and the tumor would be benign.

I jumped out of the car quickly and waved Jan goodbye. I stood alone on the corner of Charles and Pratt streets a few blocks from Baltimore's Inner Harbor.

"Andy, it's cancer."

My mind is different than most. First, it's slow. Like an old 386 computer, it takes a while for me to process things, still today. I literally stare at someone for a few seconds while they wait for me to respond. People find it off-putting. When I say people, I mean employees and my wife. Secondly, my mind tends to filter out any negativity. It doesn't allow bad things to enter.

It might be breast cancer, I thought, *but it will be the curable kind, and she'll be fine.*

A week later, we found out it was HER2/neu-positive, which was a bad cancer to have. Not only that, it was stage four, meaning it was very advanced and was already in her liver. My mind was having a hard time putting a positive spin on this information.

When I was a child Jodi was my security blanket after our biological mother died. I refused to go anywhere without her when I was a kid, not even going to birthday parties unless she was invited too. Sleepovers were painful for me.

We spent a lot of time together growing up. Of course, we did the whole sibling fighting thing, and I drove her nuts, especially hanging around all her friends in high school.

Jodi Buerger, circa 1988, at a friend's wedding wearing Brona's pearls

She went to college at Boston University, while I was only three hours away at the University of Vermont, in Burlington. We visited each other often. She'd come skiing, and I went to Boston frequently. I was on the University of Vermont Club Crew, and we often crashed at Jodi's place for regattas. After college, I lived in far-away places: Aspen, Boulder, and Vancouver. She still made time to visit. I did the same for her.

Even though Jodi was thir-teen months older, she was

technically a baby boomer. As boomers tend to do, she obsessed over getting the best possible job after graduation, regardless of the quality of life. She landed a great position in Ross Perot's Electronic Data Systems (EDS). Jodi was on the GM account and found herself in Detroit, Michigan, in 1986, not exactly a party town in those years. She hated it.

After college I helped my father out by working temporarily at one of his newspapers to cover for a woman on maternity leave in Detroit. I also hated Detroit, but I relished the chance to live under the same roof as Jodi again for the first time in six years, even if it meant sleeping on her couch for three months. We explored, worked out, and traveled. Her then-boyfriend lived out of town and visited often. I got upset, so he brought his sister along one time. We wound up dating for a few years. I relished the double dates we had that summer of 1987.

When that job was finished, I packed up, and as a Gen-Xer, I chased my best possible job—being a ski instructor in Aspen. Jodi didn't much mind visiting me there either.

After I moved to Baltimore in 1997 and Jodi had moved back to Boston, gotten married, and had children, I made trips to Boston every few months to see her. Once she received the diagnosis of advanced breast cancer, our family took turns taking her for the hard, frequent treatments required. I hated the reason I was there, but it was comforting to spend a lot of time with her.

Climb for Hope

Over the years I've become the same kind of wannabe athlete my father was. I've participated in a lot of sports, never really mastering any, save for skiing. I always like trying new things. Hiking 14,000-foot mountains in Colorado sparked me to try bigger and harder ones, such as Mount Whitney and Mount Rainier.

Hoping to become even more proficient, I took numerous mountaineering courses to learn about avalanche safety and basic skills. After all that, I struggled with the most elementary of knots. God help me if I fall into a crevasse. I'm still out on the mountains every year, though, and the guides shake their heads in disbelief that I need help putting on my crampons.

It's always fun to have Andy out on a trip."

My favorite memories of him camping are the times we harassed each other over coffee. Most campers drink instant, but Andy is a high-maintenance camper when it comes to his routine, and he has to have his coffee press. He's usually the guy who needs help setting up his tent, and usually the last guy to get his backpack packed. Andy has one set way of doing things, and sometimes it takes a lot longer than most of the other folks. He's definitely on "Andy time."

I can look at Andy one minute and he's completely clean. The next minute, I look over and he's covered in gobs and gobs of sunscreen—*way* too much. He looks like Emperor Palpatine in *Star Wars*—the character with the black hood and the face that's completely white.

—Ricky Haro
Managing Member
Rare Earth Adventures

Ricky Haro helps Andy with his pack, again, on Mount Adams

In 2005, after one of our regular climbing workouts at the Earth Treks gym, my long-time friend Eric Kronthal (Krony) and I decided to go on a climb together. We wanted a bigger mountain than either of us had ever tried. We thought, "How about something like the 18,500-foot Pico de Orizaba," the highest mountain in Mexico and the third highest in North America, after Denali and Mount Logan.

Krony found a Mexican company that could supply permits, a guide, and all the rest of the logistics. We picked a date in November.

When I left the house and got in that taxi for the airport, I left behind that relationship with Deb. We both realized we weren't right for each other.

During those two years with her, though, I learned a lot about myself. Deb was also a big advocate for people with breast cancer, and she taught me a lot about the disease. Just before Eric and I left for Mexico, I had been virtually searching the world for the best breast cancer research. Deb introduced me to a fascinating woman at The Johns Hopkins Hospital.

Dr. Leisha Emens, MD, Ph.D. was using immunotherapy to combat cancer; groundbreaking stuff. It entailed employing the body's own immune system to attack the cancer. She took a sufferer's tumor cells, turned off their DNA, chopped them up into a million pieces, and injected them back into the victim's body. She also added a very small dose of chemotherapy to help wake up the immune system. It worked fabulously in Phase I mouse trials and showed promise in early trials on humans. I loved the idea and research. I saw the ravages that chemo took on my sister and became enamored with this different approach.

"Dr. Emens, what do you need?" I asked.

She replied simply, "Money."

The expedition in Mexico was bizarre. I loved the journey. Climbing also involves a lot of downtime, which I thoroughly enjoyed with Krony in the beautiful Servimont compound owned by Dr. Reyes. In that downtime my mind also went to some bad places—the end of my relationship; we were gone during the ninth anniversary of my father's death, and finding a cure for Jodi's disease.

When you're on a mountain with an old friend for several days, you talk about the important stuff in life. I told him about my failed relationship, and I told him about Jodi's battle with cancer; that she might not survive more than another year or so. I said, "I want to find a way to mix a couple of my passions. I want to figure out how I can fundraise for some immunotherapy research at Johns Hopkins. Boy, if it would help my sister, that would be great. I need to do something, and I would like to mix that with climbing."

Krony remembers how we came up with the idea for Climb for Hope:

> We started talking about the notion of Climb for Hope and what would it take to get a busload of people on board with fundraising and climbing. I've always believed that if you want to accomplish anything you should set your goal much further than where the reasonable endpoint might be. In my own life, I always find that it's typical to fall short of grandiose goals but still meet a meaningful goal. Andy and I talked about how many people we could get to do it, and I remember thinking, if we want ten people to go on a climb, try to get a bus full, and we will probably wind up with ten.
>
> I helped Andy recruit climbers. I had a previous life in fundraising, so I helped people write the letters and reach out to

people they knew. There was more interest than I could have imagined. We thought we could find a dozen people to go, but we signed up close to twenty-five for the first Climb for Hope on Cotopaxi in Ecuador.

Krony encouraged me to approach Chris Warner and ask him to lead our first climb. Chris was the founder of Earth Treks and also led international expeditions. Chris was the ninth American to have summited both Everest and K2, the world's two highest mountains. Unlike Everest, K2 is extremely technical. Only 306 people have ever stood atop K2, whereas more than 5,600 have been on the Everest summit. Also, eighty-six have died. That's a very ugly death-to-summit ratio.

Chris Warner, one of America's most accomplished mountaineers, took us on our first three climbs, making no money so we could donate more to charity. One of the few moments he's not moving fast.

Chris graciously agreed to meet with me. Over coffee at his Columbia, Maryland, climbing gym, he suggested we head for Cotopaxi, which at 19,500 feet, is the world's highest active volcano. (It erupted a few years after we climbed it.) Chris not only agreed to take us, but he also said he would charge us only his costs, not making money on us, which would allow us to give more money to research.

We held a meeting at Earth Treks' Timonium, Maryland, gym in April 2006. Krony recruited two dozen people who packed into a room.

I had tried to take a hiatus from dating for a while until I met a beautiful redhead in February who loved reading and adventure. We hadn't been dating long, and I thought I could impress her by taking her to this really cool meeting. Her name was Jennifer.

Where's the Ring?

Do you want the rest of the story? I was thirty-two years old, I had just moved to Baltimore for a job at Johns Hopkins, and I was not about to go to a bar to meet people. Without telling me, my nurse friends posted a profile for me on Match.com, and Andy contacted me.

The first time we talked, my head was a little foggy from the prescriptions I was taking after a minor surgery, and I kept calling him Al, but Andy let it slide. I eventually got his name right, and we continued to communicate for three weeks until he asked me to a Rolling Stones concert. I declined because I felt I didn't know him well enough.

His next offer was more low-key, and also a test. Andy did not believe that I was Jewish, so he invited me on a date to his house for dinner on a Friday, which was Shavuot. I told my neighbors where I was going and instructed them, "If I'm not home by eleven, call the police."

Andy made me say the prayers, and I passed the test. We talked about our dreams and having a family. I was home by eleven.

On our second date we looked at each other and asked, "Do you want to date anyone else anymore?" We both answered, "No. I'm good."

After a few months, I decided it was time for us to get engaged. Andy was not quite there yet, but I knew I wanted to marry him, so I went with him to the meeting where he was trying to recruit climbers for Climb for Hope. I went only because I wanted to spend time with him, but I was amazed at what I discovered at that meeting. Andy is a philanthropist. I don't know anything sexier than that, and he does it outdoors. Hello! At the end of the meeting, I said to the group, "I don't know if Andy and I will be together or not, but I don't care. I am going to be on this trip."

As we spent more time together and trained together, I still did not want to climb that mountain as badly as Andy did, but I was really ready to get engaged, so he used that information to motivate me. "If you make it to the top of Cotopaxi," he told me, "we'll get engaged." I climbed 19,500 feet to the summit and waited for him to pull a little box out of his backpack, but nothing. Where's the ring? "Honey, that was just something I said," he explained. Not too long after that, though, while we were snowshoeing in Aspen, he proposed. A typical adventure for us.

—Jennifer Buerger

Finally! Here's the ring! Aspen Mountain, April 2007. (Not pictured: snowshoes)

At the meeting, Chris gave an introduction about the logistics of the trip. Chris not only held the speed record on Cotopaxi, he's also a sought-after public speaker. Leisha presented the details of her promising, exciting research. The duo wowed the crowd, and every single person attending signed up for the trip.

Leisha called me after the meeting. We had invited her to "travel with us" while in-country. There were some easier hikes she could take. I thought it would be nice for her to meet the group and inspire us. She could cheer us on and then sightsee in Ecuador.

"No, I want to climb with you," she insisted.

We left in January 2007 and traveled in Ecuador for a few days with breathtaking acclimatization hikes. The day arrived for us to head to the mountain for our summit attempt. We drove to Cotopaxi, and the bus let us off about an hour's hike away from the hut where we'd set up. We slept in bunks and made our meals there.

Chris and his trusted the Earth Treks lead guide, Dan Jenkins, had a great strategic plan for us. We took a rest day and had snow school, learning the skills we needed to climb the mountain. They broke us up into five rope teams based on our speed they witnessed during the acclimatization hikes. They were going to send us out for the summit starting at midnight, slowest to fastest. That way, they could pull sick or tired climbers off the ropes and take them down safely, without making the whole team turn around. It also afforded us the opportunity for all of us to reach the summit at about the same time.

Lt. Dan can be very nurturing. He can also be a little gruff on the rope.

Even though it took place more than a decade ago, I have vivid images of our climb up Cotopaxi. I was one of the few experienced climbers, having done many expeditions before, including an unsuccessful attempt on that very mountain.

Chris chose Michelle Timmerman, Ashley Worden, Jennifer, and me to rope in together. As with all first-timers, they were petrified. I tied in fifth, bringing up the rear. Dan tied in at the front of the climbing rope. Dan, who has become a good friend, is a very experienced international climber. He's also a fantastic coach and guide. He was nurturing in preparing for our goal, offering helpful hints every day. "Make slow, deliberate movements," he reminded us. "It's like putting pennies in your jar, saving up for the summit push."

He can also be gruff when he needs to get your attention on the mountain. Early into the trip, he earned the nickname Lieutenant Dan, after the *Forest Gump* character.

Ashley described him as "encouraging and uplifting. He carried the weight of the team, especially when he took on Michelle's pack as well as his. Experienced. Trustworthy."

We received a lot of coaching on the ascent. We received our share of loud "constructive criticism" as well. Cue *Forrest Gump* reel.

Having trained extremely hard, we traveled at a pace comfortable for me. Michelle had some altitude-related issues and was taken down, but the rest of our rope made it to the summit. One climber, Kathi Levine, vomited when she left the hut and didn't attempt the summit. Two other climbers had altitude challenges and went down with Michelle, but everyone else from the five other rope teams succeeded as well.

Chris's strategy worked. Four teams were on the summit at the same time. We didn't see the fifth team though. The fifth team, dubbed the "slow rope," had Leisha, Gary Raffel, and Gary Ingber. Leisha attacked that mountain like she did her research: singularly focused on her goal until she succeeded. Speed wasn't her thing. Despite the slow pace, she asked the guide to slow down, to which guide "Big Eric" replied, "If we go any slower, we'll decompose."

Not taking anything away from the quinquagenarian Garys, we really wanted Leisha on that summit. We worried that the group wasn't going to make it. We couldn't get them on the radio. We were getting cold up there and couldn't wait any longer. We had a big celebration with hugs and lots of photos. Only slightly damped by the missing slow rope, we knew it was time to descend. Just as we tied in again and readied to leave, there on the crest was the final rope team. They all made it. Joel Shalowitz shed lots of tears, later claiming he got sunscreen in his eyes.

Overall it was a successful first fundraising expedition. We raised $150,000 and got twenty of twenty-four people safely to the summit and back.

Mount Shasta's Initials are MS

Poor Jonny Guth, or Gunner, as we call him, worked hard on the Cotopaxi expedition. He trained like a machine. He was strong. In fact, it was quickly apparent that Jon was stronger and faster up the mountains than anyone else on the team during the three acclimatization hikes we did in Ecuador before taking on all 19,400 feet of the country's second tallest mountain after Chimborazo. Jonny was the fastest guy on the fast rope that trip. Not only that, but he also contributed tremendously to getting Climb for Hope off the ground.

A Greater Calling

To me it was one of the more interesting things to see how people will push themselves and force themselves to do something entirely unfamiliar—like climbing up a glacier in the middle of the night to get to a summit in the first light of the morning—for a greater purpose.

Most of the time mountaineering is a pretty self-centered ambition, but when you make it unselfish, when you make it about somebody other than yourself, it is inspirational. Seeing everybody's face as they reached the top of Cotopaxi left an indelible imprint on me. It's something I will never forget—seeing people do something they would never have dreamed of, had there not been a greater calling or cause.

—Eric Kronthal

"Krony" strikes a pose on the summit of Mount Cotopaxi

He helped create our website, built out all our IT infrastructure, and recruited climbers. All those things contributed a huge part to our early success.

During the seven days on Cotopaxi, however, Gunner was the first person hit by illness. Down goes Gunner. He succumbed to a bug that required him to be near a bathroom at all times. We quarantined him, long before COVID-19 made quarantine a thing. Fortunately, he got it early and managed to recover in time to leave for the mountain. After raising more than $5,000, training, performing administration work, and undergoing acclimatization hikes in-country, he was on-mountain.

On what was supposed to be a rest day at the hut, Chris Warner took that opportunity to hold "snow school," where we learned all the skills we needed to do the technical climbing. He taught us how to put on crampons and walk around on the steep ice. He taught us how to use our ice axes to self-arrest, or in other words, stop sliding downhill before we fell into a crevasse. But you don't ever practice the sliding self-arrest while actually wearing the crampons. Unless you're Gunner. The super-hyper, no-fear guy tried, and he snapped his ankle. Gunner was done, twelve hours before the team left for our summit attempt. Twelve hours! Twelve hours before his birthday. Yes, we were supposed to summit on Gunner's birthday. But Gunner wasn't coming. He was going home with a broken leg…in a wheelchair.

I'm not sure who felt worse, Gunner or me.

He begged me to take him on another climb soon after Cotopaxi. I couldn't say no. His leg was in a cast for two months. We settled on climbing again in June, three months later, and two full weeks before his first child was due to be born.

We chose Mount Shasta, a 14,000-foot volcano in Northern California, forty miles south of the Oregon border. Getting there was an expedition in itself, but Jennifer, Jonny, and our friend Julie went out there for a long weekend.

We had no guides, so we carried everything up to base camp. It was tough and beautiful. Despite the physical challenge, Jennifer loved every minute of it. Shasta was a quaint western town. The views of and from the mountain were spectacular. The air was fresh and clean; we had a reprieve from the oppressive Baltimore humidity. We worked our way through the delicious pine forest.

We arrived at our camp in the early afternoon with plenty of time to set up tents, melt snow to make water, and prepare dinner before an early bedtime. June 1, 2007, was a warm, sunny afternoon. It's an odd feeling at nine thousand feet where you're walking on snow that is cold but the heat of the sun can make you uncomfortably hot. Jon, Julie, and I wore shorts and T-shirts. Jennifer was freezing. We couldn't get her to warm up. She had similar issues on our winter training hikes in Vermont and our acclimatization hikes in Ecuador, so she put on all her cold-weather gear, including a hat, gloves, and a down jacket. We then put her in the tent inside a sleeping bag rated to zero degrees. She was still shivering.

At six p.m. we all got in our bags inside our tents to get a few hours of "sleep" before our alpine start at midnight. We had to get up and down before the snow got too soft and difficult to hike through. I said good night to Jennifer. She wasn't feeling one hundred percent.

She asked me, "Andy, do you mind if I skip the summit? I'm happy here."

Climbing for me is always about safety, not the summit. I wouldn't take anyone who had any doubts. "Of course," I replied.

For Jennifer the climbing experience was about getting outside and enjoying the views from incredible heights. She was going to spend the morning at base camp taking it all in. That was fine.

Jon, Julie, and I woke up at 11:30 p.m. and were on our way at midnight to the summit to catch the sunrise at six a.m. Jon, who had been inactive for months, wasn't at his peak endurance. Still, after a longer ascent than we expected, we made our way to the summit.

The last stretch of any climb is hard. You're tired; you keep thinking the summit is just a few yards away, and it's not. It's also normally a steep section. It's cold.

Compounding those obstacles was that Shasta is a volcano. The vents release a sulfurous gas. There's nothing like gasping for breath only to get a huge whiff of rotten egg odor. We pushed through the smell and the last steep, rocky stretch in time for a breathtaking sunrise. We took it all in, snapped some photos, and turned around.

The last one thousand vertical feet on the descent into camp is Avalanche Gulch. It's steep. We were coming down that final glacier before base camp delighted to see Jennifer packing up camp for us. We had a red-eye to catch home, and every minute was helpful. We watched her for a while. Jennifer was new to climbing and didn't have all the skills yet. For example, she took the stakes out from the tent to pack it up. A big gust of wind came and blew the tent off the cliff and down five hundred feet below us.

I fetched the tent.

As we all climbed down, Jennifer decided to save time and energy by doing her favorite activity: glissading. In glissading you sit on your butt and slide down the mountain using your ice axe to control your speed. Jennifer loved it. She was losing altitude rapidly without expending energy, managing also to soak up the surroundings.

Jonny, on the other hand, wasn't able to slide, either because his fifty-pound pack was dragging, or his pants weren't conducive. Regardless, he grew frustrated. He taught us a few new words on that descent, but nothing could yuck Jen's yum.

We went into town and stopped at a little pub that served delicious hamburgers that we washed down with some great local ale. We sat outside in the shadow of our accomplishment. The Northern California air was dry and comfortable. It was neither hot nor cold. That was in stark contrast with Baltimore's hot, sticky nights. We weren't sure Jennifer was going to board that flight. She was pretty at home in that hippie town, one town over from Weed, California.

She did come home. She came home with a smile on her face and amazing memories. That was her second big expedition in six months.

A month later in July, Jennifer's foot dropped. She couldn't control it. We were both frightened. She got an appointment with an orthopedic surgeon a month away. No! I got on the horn and called every orthopedic surgeon I could. We were able to get an appointment the following week.

A few days after we booked that appointment, Jennifer called me at my office. Something was wrong. "I got into a little car accident. I'm fine. My back is tightening up a little, but I'm fine," she said. "It was a little fender bender. We weren't going that fast."

"Jen, I'll meet you at Sinai Hospital in fifteen minutes," I told her. "Goodbye."

By the time I got there, the staff had taken her to a room, and I saw her lying there in excruciating pain. The doctors wanted to run a bunch of tests, take an MRI of her back, and keep her overnight for observation.

I may not have been the world's best boyfriend, and we were engaged to be married in two months. I figured out quickly that I needed to sleep in the chair in her room.

A nice neurologist appeared in the room early the next morning. (I'm glad I was there.) He told us the MRI looked good. No visible damage on her back. She would be fine.

The doctor then slipped in, "I did see a tiny spot on your spine. The good news is that it's not cancer."

"What else could it be?" Jennifer and I yelled.

"It could be MS, but MS means multiple sclerosis or multiple lesions, and we see just one tiny spot. Let's keep an eye on it. Get an MRI every ninety days just to be safe," said the nice neurologist.

We eloped to Kennebunk, Maine, and were married overlooking the river on September 30, 2007. There were just ten of us—Jen's parents and their good friends, my mom, Jodi, my best friend Alan, and my dear friend/rabbi/drinking coach Steve Schwartz.

Jennifer and I stayed in Maine for a few more days for a honeymoon. There were no hiking or major outdoor adventures. Jen's back was still wrecked, and she could barely walk. There was a lot of Scrabble playing. We did manage to go whale watching.

Having kids right away was out of the question with her back in that kind of shape. She couldn't carry a loaf of bread, so carrying a baby wasn't going to happen.

We went dog shopping in-
stead. We fought over breeds
for a while and settled on a
bullmastiff, which we both fell
in love with when we visited
a breeder. They got to be 140
pounds of drooling, wrinkly
love. We couldn't wait for the
puppy to arrive. We put down
the first deposit, so we got the
pick of the litter.

She had her next MRI the following month. All clear.

*"MS was going to be something positive
in our lives." Puppy Mt Shasta at 8 weeks.*

The next MRI was in February 2008. I then took off for a guys' ski trip
in Whitefish, Montana. Man, I needed that. A vacation, hard skiing, a
few beers, and male bonding.

Jennifer was kind enough to pick me up at the airport when I got home.
She seemed a little off. Halfway through the thirty-minute drive, we
passed the Baltimore Harbor, and Jennifer blurted out, "They found
another lesion, and they think it's MS."

I think she meant to say, "Welcome home, dear. How was your trip?"

She had scheduled a doctor's appointment for the next day. On
February 26, 2008, we sat in the University of Maryland's MS center
waiting for the doctor. It was three days shy of our five-month anniversary. Even though we *knew* the result, the wait was excruciating.
We sat in silence. I fidgeted with the gadget I'd recently bought. (It

allowed me to get emails on my cellphone. It was called a Blackberry.) I read through an email that arrived. It said, "Congratulations, Andy! Your puppy was just born."

"Mrs. Buerger, the doctor will see you now," the nurse called out.

We went home and cried ourselves to sleep that night hugging each other in the terror of the unknown.

The next morning we woke up and named our new bullmastiff: Mount Shasta, or MS for short. It was a beautiful town that Jennifer adored. It was the last mountain we climbed together, and damn it, MS was going to be something positive in our lives. February 28 is known as MS Day in our house.

We hated the doctor at the University of Maryland. He told us to pick what drug we wanted her to be on and see him again in six months. No. Not acceptable. This was a serious, lifelong affliction. Jennifer needed an expert and someone with some sense of bedside manner.

Our research showed that Johns Hopkins Medical University had "The best MS treatment center in the country," and Dr. Peter Calabresi was The Man to see there. I called and got an appointment…in six months. There was high demand and not enough resources to help everyone in a timely manner.

Still, that schedule wasn't going to work. She needed attention now.

I sent an email to what seemed like my entire database, asking for help getting us in to see Dr. Calabresi. The next day my phone rang.

"Hello. Dr. Calabresi can squeeze you in next Wednesday," said the voice on the other end.

In shock, I had to ask, "Thank you so much, and who told you about us?"

"Dr. Leisha Emens," she answered. Of course. Karma. We had an appointment to squeeze in to see Dr. Calabresi, but he spent an hour with us answering every silly question we had.

"Look," Dr. Calabresi started, "your disease is progressing quickly, which I don't like. I can keep you out of a wheelchair, though."

Unlike the cold, distant doc who just laid the bad news on us and virtually kicked us out of his office, Dr. Calabresi reviewed our drug options for more than an hour with a quiet, sad, and compassionate voice as if he were telling his wife the news. MS drugs don't cure the disease the way some cancer drugs can. Drugs only possibly prevent MS from getting worse. Some drugs aren't as effective, allowing the disease to still progress. The more lesions you get, the worse your symptoms become. Pain. Fatigue. Numbness. Loss of use of your limbs. Too many lesions on your spine equals a wheelchair.

We finally chose a treatment. That's when Dr. Calabresi said to us, "You'll have to go on this drug right away," and that meant we couldn't get pregnant.

Some people dream about being a doctor or president of the United States. Rich. Famous. Jen wanted to be a mother. That was her *why*. That's why she was put on this earth: to use all her nurturing skills and abilities to raise emotionally and physically healthy kids. It took all my energy to convince her to get on that drug and embark on a new quest for an alternate way to become a mother. We explored everything from surrogacy to adoption.

The Flags of Kilimanjaro

After our overwhelmingly successful first fundraising climb on Cotopaxi, the entire team couldn't wait to get back on another mountain. It was a life-changing experience for every volunteer fundraising climber.

We had no plans. When we started the organization, we wouldn't have dreamed we'd amass $150,000 in one year. Nor did we foresee how moved people would be by raising promising money for breast cancer research. We all climbed up the world's highest active volcano and descended as changed people.

What next for the tight-knit group? One of the famed Seven Summits, like Mount Elbrus in Russia? Climbing the Seven Summits meant climbing the highest peak on each continent. That would be fun and hold a lot of marketing appeal. There was, however, a little military dustup at the Russia/Georgia border. Next?

Before we found out Jennifer had MS, she had voted for Kilimanjaro, another of the famed Seven Summits. She was always obsessed with Africa, even minoring in it at the University of Kansas. For me it was too easy. I wanted another technical mountain. Jennifer thought it was a chance to finally get to Africa for an epic adventure and perhaps go on safari.

We chose Kilimanjaro.

The big downside was that we had to wait a torturous eighteen months to climb again because we climbed Cotopaxi in January, and the best climbing season for Kili is June—too soon to prepare and fundraise for that same year. Our group had grown so close that it was miserable ticking off the months until the following June.

The trip filled up immediately. Chris Warner from Earth Treks was kind enough to give us a second group. Thirty people. Thirty people would climb Kili with us on two expeditions. I went on the second.

By the time we left, we raised another $250,000 for breast cancer research.

We were all glad the moment arrived. Simultaneously we were all disappointed that Jennifer's MS had progressed to a point that prevented her from going. Saying goodbye to Jennifer was gut wrenching. Kili was her idea, her dream, and our dream to go together. It wasn't fair that she couldn't come. Her recovery became another hope for me to climb for.

We landed in Arusha in June 2008.

Kili looms large over the horizon. Mount Everest, the highest mountain on any continent, rises above its neighboring mountains by only a few thousand feet, so you can't see much of it. Everest was created by tectonic plates coming together pushing up the earth. Kili, on the other hand, is a volcano that stands alone. A whopping 15,000 of its 19,400 feet are visible above the earth.

The trek involved going up a winding path for six days, including one day off for rest. We would then descend in two days. We were all in outstanding shape, but you never know how a body will respond to altitude. We were all taking Diamox, a prescription drug normally used to treat glaucoma. It also helps prevent altitude sickness.

We didn't have to carry heavy packs. That job fell on the local porters. We carried only our food, water, and clothing for the day. We also carried flags in our packs. Someone carried the flag with the Climb for Hope logo. I carried two flags—one to support Jennifer and one that read Stay Strong, JB, to remind Jodi we were working to find a cure for her; please hang in there. Others carried the names of people who died from breast cancer or people undergoing treatment. We carried the flags as reminders of why we were there every step of the way, and hoped we would get an opportunity to get our pictures taken with them at the summit.

Camping below the Barranco Wall on Mount Kilimanjaro for 36 hours gave the team a much-needed rest day, but psyched them out having to stare at the most technical section of the expedition

One of the many fascinating things about Kili is that you hike through five climatic zones. We started out like rabbits running up through the first rainy wet zone. There was another expedition starting along with us. We saw them every day. One day they'd walk past us; another we'd be faster and go ahead of them. We were friendly and chatted sometimes.

Everyone seemed to be in shape and adjusting well to the altitude. We made our way slowly up the mountain. The local guides reminded us every few hours: "*Polepole*," they'd shout, meaning "slowly" in Swahili. Each day we could literally see our goal above and set our minds on it. The summit got closer and closer. The group spent day four as a rest day just below the Barranco Wall. The spot is beautiful but daunting. Navigating up the wall is the most technical part of the expedition, and we were forced to stare at it for thirty-six hours without letting it psych us out. It managed to spook a few of us.

As we started up the wall on day five, most people got nervous scrambling up the rocks and with sheer drops just feet away. The Kenyan guides once again provided simple, sage advice. "Set your mind to free," uttered Davis, the lead African guide.

We were never sure if he misspoke the English phrase "Set your mind free" or was just very profound. Didn't matter. We loved it. After a difficult day, we reached our high camp with our minds at free, just four thousand vertical feet below the famed summit.

We had the normal challenges to be expected along the way. Day one we watched Lieutenant Dan sprint for the first outhouse he saw, cutting in the line. A few people fell ill with altitude sickness, losing their lunch along the way.

Things got real for me at high camp. Camping at 15,000 feet isn't easy. It's noticeably colder. The campsite was littered with rockfall, which makes walking around difficult. The thin air often left me suddenly gasping for breath while just sitting still.

The other group we were leapfrogging for five days was up there as well.

The goal was no longer in sight, which was hard. We needed our goal for inspiration. We camped below the massive peak and couldn't see the top. We huddled in the cook tent for a warm dinner and to plot our strategy for the summit push.

Lieutenant Dan came back as the lead climb and endeared himself to everyone again. He wanted all twenty-four of us to leave at the same time but broke us into sub-teams that would stick together. I was with Amy and the Midei family—Mark, Denise, and daughter Allie. We'd depart at eleven p.m. and hike through the night. At midnight it would be Mark's birthday, and I quietly hoped he wouldn't have the Gunner birthday curse. Allie had been vomiting her way to high camp. Mark had the same problem on Cotopaxi. Amy wasn't particularly strong. I kept my concerns to myself.

"Thousands of donors are watching us"

We "slept" in our tents for a few hours before being called into the cook tent for our 11:30 p.m. breakfast. Lieutenant Dan called on me to give remarks before heading out into the dark, cold night into a world of pain.

"Gang," I started, "thank you. Thank you for all you've done to this point." I went on to say, "We're successful already, and we haven't left the tent. We raised $250,000 for breast cancer research at Johns

Hopkins. We sped up research on an important vaccine by six months. That alone will save countless lives. Congratulations!"

Tears filled my eyes. "Please. Please do me a favor. My sister is battling stage four breast cancer back home. Keep her in your hearts and minds. Carry her to the summit with you. Carry your loved ones who are battling cancer. Take them to the summit with you. Show them we can do this. We can overcome obstacles. Carry the spirit of those we lost to this horrible disease. We'll be 19,400 feet closer to them."

I paused to keep from completely breaking down in sobs.

"The thousands of donors are watching us. The people battling cancer are watching us. Let's get those flags to the summit for them, because they can't. We're climbing for the people who can't. My wife, Jennifer, can no longer climb. We can. If for some reason you have to turn around, please make sure you hand your flag to someone who can get it there. Let's get a picture of the flags at the summit."

I gave one final plea before we turned on the headlamps and started the journey. "We're going to get altitude sickness and vomit. These packs will get heavy. Our legs will be tired. But Jodi and all cancer sufferers deal with nausea and fatigue every, single, day. They feel like they're carrying backpacks twenty-four hours a day, seven days a week, 365 days a year. We can do it for eighteen hours."

The twenty-four climbers filed out of the tent with our headlamps illuminated. Two dozen people started putting one foot in front of the other—for hours. Allie threw up. We walked mostly without talking, conserving energy and ensuring deep breaths. I took the Ray Lewis approach. I periodically pierced the silence and screamed encouragement. "We got this." Or "We're strong. Nothing is stopping us. This mountain is ours."

At midnight we all sang happy birthday to Mark Midei under labored breath.

Parts of that top climbing section are blurs to me. I can't recall many details. I dissociated. The fatigue. I do remember the extreme cold. The cold made me slightly hypothermic. I climbed with my huge down jacket on. That jacket had gotten me through the coldest moments of my life. I had never climbed in it. It was too hot, but this time I couldn't even get warm trekking in that down coat.

We stopped every sixty minutes for a ten-minute break. In that short time we had to pee, drink water, force down some calories, and add layers. The thing was, I had no more layers to add. I got even colder when we stopped moving. Lieutenant Dan screamed at us like we were in basic training. "Let's go! Get those packs back on and start walking. Come on! This is taking too long."

I also remember cresting the last slope to the caldera. It was gorgeous, yet there was little time to view it. Things became a bit of a goat rodeo from there. False summits are tricky. You think you're there, and despite not having a huge amount of vertical to conquer, it's still an hour's walk to the real summit. The sub-groups disintegrated, and it was every person for himself for the final hour.

Other things I can vaguely remember:

- We had to huddle on top of one female to get her core body temperature up.
- That's where the trail got icy, and without crampons, walking was treacherous.
- Michael Ingber, who was only seventeen and climbing with his fifty-nine-year-old father, Gary, was struggling. He couldn't stand up—a combination sheer fatigue and the fact that his

boots were unable to grip the ice—but his body wouldn't quit. He kept putting one foot in front of the other. I'm not sure if it was me or other people holding Michael up so he wouldn't slip on the ice.

- The famed snows of Kilimanjaro were finally visible. I tried to appreciate the glacier. I knew I'd likely never be there again, and if I were, the snows probably wouldn't. I tried to imprint them in my mind for future generations, to tell my unborn kids someday.

"Wait. There it is! There's the famous wooden sign. That's the summit," I told myself.

Highest Point in Africa, the sign read.

We made it. We made it. We all made it. Hugs. Tears. Photos. The flags. All the flags made it, along with all twenty-four climbers and our guides.

We all made it to the summit of Mount Kilimanjaro with our flags!

"Stay Strong, JB."

"Climb for Hope."

"We love you, Jen."

"Thank you."

And then just like that, we descended. It took a measly one and a half days to go down what took us six days to go up. Our leapfrogging friends were on the way down too.

I do have memories of coming off the summit. I lost everyone. I hiked down by myself. My boots were one size too small and banged my big toes with every step for hours. My knees hurt with ever step as well.

I stumbled back into camp. Emotions overwhelmed me. I thought of Jodi, Jennifer, my father who would have been proud, my own accomplishment, and the incredible team effort. I grabbed the satellite phone and called my wife. I was crying so hard Jennifer couldn't understand me. Jennifer should have been there. I did this bucket list feat without my best friend. Life wasn't fair. I missed her so much. So many miles separated us. I just wanted to share this accomplishment with her. I wanted a hug from her.

I collected myself. I was the leader. We needed to celebrate this victory. I made sure I welcomed, hugged, and thanked every climber coming down. We did it for those who couldn't. Many tears were shed by many people in honor of the people we climbed for and for those who had lost the battle.

The next day we made it down and out. We stayed at a really nice

Dr. Leisha Emens and Andy after getting their flags to the summit of Kilimanjaro

hotel. We managed a shower and then cocktails on the patio outside the restaurant. A fire burned in a pit. Over a beer I finally had the opportunity to chat with a member of the other climbing group. "How'd it go for y'all?" I asked.

"Okay, I guess. Twelve of our twenty-four summited," one guy replied. "Well, Tom got tired, so Sue took him down. Rachael's feet got cold, so Bob took her down."

"Um. Okay," was all I said out loud.

To myself I was screaming, "Are you kidding me? You turned around when your feet got cold or you got tired?"

Look, I'm a very safe climber, but how are those things going to stop you?

We had a mission: We had flags with loved one's names on them in our packs that had to get to the summit. Our logo was on one. My sister's name was on one. Thousands of people were counting on us. Turning around when our feet got cold wasn't an option.

That lesson stuck with me. It became part of who I am. Carry a flag. Know your mission.

I got back home a week later from a fantastic expedition to the summit of Africa's highest peak. Our trip was successful before we left, raising $250,000. All twenty-four of my climbers braved the horrible cold, altitude sickness, stomach distress, dehydration, and exhaustion. I'm proud of each one of them. They learned that mountaineering is a team sport and they learned so much about themselves. It was a beautiful, fun, challenging, rewarding, and emotional group journey.

Know Your Why

We quickly discovered that Climb for Hope brought together many people of different ages, backgrounds, professions, climbing experiences, and interests. And all of a sudden you're all on a mountain with the same exact goal in mind, united under one flag, one mission. Workplaces can be like that. An ideal organization cherishes and celebrates diversity to get a variety of experiences and opinions. Your flag or mission gets everyone going in the same direction. You can overcome many obstacles on your way to your goal when that flag is in your pack.

As Mark Twain said, finding out your *why*, or your mission/purpose in life, is life-changing. When your *why* is big enough, you can overcome any *how*. Your team will dig deep, work together, and think strategically to reach its goal.

"That guy with the vision"

Andy is that guy with the vision and the ability to get others to join in the parade. He leads by example—the first one up in the morning and the last one to bed after everybody else is snoozing away in their tents.

—Tiger Beaudoin
Entrepreneur and Jodi's Climb for Hope volunteer

"The best sister in the world"

I saw a cure coming in 2010. I was going to will it so. I repeated the mantra over and over, every day in the mirror: "We will have a cure for HER2/neu-positive breast cancer in 2010." Jodi needed to hang on for just two more years. She kept having setbacks, and she, along with great doctors, kept overcoming them.

We had reason to believe that we were making a difference. We raised $400,000 and sped up Dr. Emens's research by six months. We achieved it by cutting her grant time and generating a lot of PR to help her find more participants for her clinical trial.

We were hard at work planning our 2009 climbs in the fall of 2008.

My best friend, Alan Fleischmann, who's more like my brother, called me to meet him in Montgomery County, Maryland, near where he lived. Strange. Jen insisted that she join us. Alan was often busy, and spontaneous one-on-one time was a luxury. We sat down at a Bethesda cafe.

Alan was tasked with telling me. They knew I wouldn't be able to handle it. Someone had to tell me to my face.

My filter didn't allow the prospect of bad news to enter my brain. Jodi was going to live. I couldn't handle or fathom life without her. She had always been there for me, through everything. Everything.

"Andy," Alan started, "Jodi's cancer has spread dramatically. They can't stop it. She doesn't have long to live."

"But that's not possible. She looks great. She's doing great," I interrupted.

"No, Andy. This is it. She has just a few more months," Alan told me.

It took a few minutes for my 386 processor to handle the data and another few minutes for the information to get through my positivity filter. Reality then sunk in.

A month went by, though, and then two. The third month was February. I decided to hop on a plane to Boston to visit. I wasn't able to get there until almost midnight. I sneaked into the house very quietly, yet of course there was my sister, waiting up for me in the kitchen. She had lost a lot of weight. She had only a little bit of hair. We chatted for a few minutes before she retired.

I spent a few days up there doing the usual things—playing with her three children and going to their sports practices. Sunday night rolled around, and I needed to head back to the airport. I had about thirty minutes before I had to leave. We were upstairs in her room.

Jodi had many gifts, but opening up was not one of them, nor was allowing people into her personal space. "Here, sit," she said, motioning to her bed.

All those years of her screaming to get out of her room rolled through my head. I sat.

We didn't say much. We just talked. In the movies there are always emotional speeches when you say that final goodbye. Jodi didn't go for that kind of stuff. I didn't need to say anything. She knew how much I loved her and how much she meant to me. My actions over forty years spoke for me.

She walked me downstairs to the front door. Tears poured down our faces. I hugged her goodbye and left. Neither of us acknowledged reality, but we both knew what it meant.

Eight weeks later we received a call that Jodi had fallen and broken her hip. Jennifer and I immediately flew to see her at the hospital. She was heavily sedated and went in and out of consciousness.

The doctors made it clear that there wasn't much that could be done, just try to make her as comfortable as possible. She couldn't be moved because of her hip. All we could do was wait. It should be a matter of days.

Jen whispered to me, "I think Jodi should be the first person to hear our news."

It took Jen and me a full year of research, discussions, arguments, and marriage counseling to reach an agreement on how we were going to have children.

Jodi opened her eyes and looked at us. She was alert.

"Jodi," I stammered. "We're going to adopt a baby from Ethiopia."

We brought a smile to her face and tears to our eyes. "What should we name it?" I asked her.

"Ethan," she suggested.

She closed her eyes and nodded off. We told her she was the best sister in the world and that we loved her. We had our alone time with Jodi to say our goodbyes. We stayed there for five days waiting, and then Jennifer and I had to get back home.

Over the next week we had updates that nothing had changed. I was supposed to fly back there on Friday, May 9, to take my turn at helping at the hospital. Alan called me at two a.m. on Thursday, May 8. I was going to Boston for a different reason and with my dark suit again.

"Some yogurt-like thing"

A month after Jodi's death, I was still reeling when we left for our next adventure. We had started Climb for Hope, now renamed Jodi's Climb for Hope in my sister's memory, and had outstanding experiences at the 19,400-foot mountains—both Cotopaxi and Kilimanjaro (only four feet of altitude difference). Chris Warner from Earth Treks came up with the creative idea of heading to Iceland in June 2009 for our next climb. Who the hell wanted to go to Iceland? Certainly not

Jen and Andy in Iceland. "We couldn't get her to leave!"

my wife, until we got to Iceland, then we couldn't get her to leave. Jen, whose MS was advanced at that point, could tag along on the expedition because we mostly car camped. She loved it, as did every single person who's ever been to Iceland.

We were taking a few hikes before tackling the Hvannadalshnúkur (seven thousand feet), which involved a mind-boggling 6,800 vertical feet, going from the sea a half mile away to the summit, which is the highest point in Iceland. Crazy.

In addition to Warner, we had a local Icelandic guide, Ivar Finnbogason. Like Chris, who held the speed record on Cotopaxi, Ivar held the speed record on Hvannadalshnúkur. We had two record-holding rabbits leading the way up to Iceland's highest peak, yet our group was slow. Painfully slow, likely making the climb an eighteen-hour ordeal.

I fueled up at breakfast.

The leaders served us some yogurt-like thing with granola. I'm lactose intolerant, but I also needed four thousand calories in my belly that day. I mean, what's a little GI distress in camp? I had put a little of the yogurt on my granola as a test two days earlier. My wife, with whom I was sharing a tent, was more averse to my taking the risk. "Andy," she squawked with a look that could kill, "I know you are starving, but you can't eat it. I can't share a tent with you if you eat that."

Being hungry wasn't an option. I ate it, and astonishingly, I was fine.

I put a little more on my granola the next day. I was a little more than fine. Everything was moving a little better, if you get my drift, so I asked Ivar, "Dude, what is this stuff?"

He showed me the cup and said, "It's not yogurt; it's skyr. Technically it's a form of cheese."

The strained "yogurt" is very similar to Greek-style yogurt but is even higher in protein and creamier. The 5.3-ounce cup we ate had twenty-two grams of protein, no added sugar, and no bad fat. I'd later learn that the probiotics consumed the lactose. Many American yogurts add skim milk powder back in for a better taste, which is why I couldn't eat most American yogurts.

By that time in my life I was full-on into my healthy lifestyle. My passion for it hadn't waned in the decade since I started, and I had always been searching for a convenient source of protein with no added sugar or toxic chemicals. It didn't exist. My mind was always working, coming up with inventions for healthy products. My poor nieces, Jessie, Calli, and Caroline, were forced to eat Uncle Andy's creations every time they visited. In 2004 the girls were only about six years old. I served them protein powder in their pancakes, muffins; faux chocolate pudding, soy yogurt, and stevia, and I made them hot chocolate from chocolate protein powder, hot water, and stevia. They didn't love coming to my house.

Interestingly, in 2014 all those products flooded the market. My friends at Kodiak Cakes sell tens of millions of dollars' worth a year. I blame my nieces for my having missed that boat. If they had only encouraged me rather than complained...

In Iceland, though, I found my product: skyr. I looked at my wife, and she knew I knew. She knew I was nutty enough to do it myself.

"My Life's Calling"

With all the health issues in his family, Andy is extremely concerned and watchful of what goes into his body. When we came home from Iceland, he got the idea that skyr could be a healthy food for the masses. He looked at me and said, "Oh my gosh, I just found my life's calling." We found the one company in the U.S. that sold it and went to work in our kitchen.

—Jennifer Buerger

The problem was that I knew nothing about skyr, yogurt, or the dairy business, and then I remembered, "When your *why* is big enough, you can overcome any *how*. I had my big *why*, and it was time to find my *how*.

We returned home in late June, and my mind was racing. How? How? How? Maybe I'd import the skyr from Iceland. Greek yogurt had just gotten hot in America. It was a great opportunity, until I saw our Icelandic skyr brand on the shelves at Whole Foods Market. Damn it!

If you can't beat 'em, join 'em. Jennifer would buy skyr by the case every week at Whole Foods. The guy who stocked the shelves was always helpful. Jen and I experimented with various flavors, differing amounts of stevia, and alternate consistencies. We gave it a protein base and figured out how to make it organic.

With our fast-paced life, we needed a healthy food we could enjoy on the go. We thought, *Let's make it drinkable,* and B'more Organic was born in our blender. It was the revolution—yogurt was growing in popularity, but there were no drinkable yogurts on the shelves at the time. We whipped up smoothies every morning with frozen fruit. They were delicious and nutritious, and the timing was perfect.

We were missing a huge part of the puzzle: where the heck we were going to make this stuff? Our kitchen wasn't an option.

I called local dairies and yogurt makers. They were either too small to take on our project or too big to want to deal with our small quantity. I ran into many dead ends. I'd call someone, get a "no," but ask for a referral, and call that person.

After months of this lack of progress, I called a farmer in Lancaster, Pennsylvania. He said, "I can't make it, but the farmer across the street, Roman Stolzfus, probably can." Expecting another dead end, I called Roman.

"Oh, you need to talk to Noah Dan," Roman replied in his thick Amish accent.

Yup, another wild goose chase.

"Okay, how do I do that?" I asked.

"I'll set up a meeting. But I warn you: Noah speaks five languages, and none of them are English."

I asked Dr. Frank Lee, a dairy scientist from my alma mater, the University of Vermont, to consult with me on the production process. He joined me a week later at the small plant Noah built on Roman's farm. Noah founded Pitango Gelato, a chain of organic gelato stores in Maryland. Gelato required a lot of organic cream. To get cream, you start with whole milk and separate the cream, leaving skim milk—a lot of skim milk. Whole milk is only ten percent cream. Noah was pouring the skim milk down the drain. He was excited to hear we wanted to pay him for his trash.

The meeting began.

Dr. Frank Lee was born in Hong Kong and still had his Chinese accent, along with a significant stutter. Roman spoke in the sing-song Amish dialect of Pennsylvania Dutch, an offshoot of German. I could barely make out what Noah was saying, as Roman had warned me, due to his strong Israeli accent.

The journey started.

Roman, the farmer, was ahead of his time. He was an early adopter of organic farming, starting in 1987. The cows always had access to grazing and were not kept in pens like most dairy cows. They ate actual grass, which is what they're supposed to eat, not grain, which is cheap. Grass-fed cows not only are healthy animals; they also produce healthier milk. The natural process of consuming grass allows the cow to produce an important nutrient, omega 3 fatty acids, which are critical to healthy human bodies. Consuming grain is bad for cows, making them sicker, which creates a vicious cycle of poor health and antibiotic use. And it makes for less nutrient-dense milk.

You don't want the cows eating grass laced with herbicides or pesticides, which is why I was overjoyed at the sight of Roman's fields when I pulled in for my first visit. The cows were in the fields eating grass. With the cows were hundreds of chickens, roaming free. The chickens ate the grubs out of the cow dung, which is what chickens naturally eat, yet most American farmers feed grain to chickens as well.

As if this location wasn't already perfect, Roman was in the process of installing solar panels on the roof of Noah's production facility, so much of the power was sustainable. From sustainable plant in a sustainable farm we were buying delicious, organic, grass-fed milk that had been previously been poured down the drain.

It was all coming together. We baked our core values into the company, and we were living them. B'more Healthy. B'more Giving. B'more Green. B'more Organic.

We ran into a new problem. I was still struggling to find a simple bottle. I couldn't find one anywhere. Roadblock. I hated to bug Dr. Lee for so much, and I hated for him to bill me, but I broke down and called him. "Frank, I can't find a source for bottles anywhere. Any suggestions?" I asked.

"I don't know. There's a bottling company down the street from my house. It's called Shelburne Plastics. Call them," Frank replied matter-of-factly.

Instead of calling, I Googled it. It turned out the company had a second plant close to the Baltimore airport, only thirty minutes from our house. Crazy! I called right away and the company agreed to sell me the bottles that were "left over" from a much larger company. I showed up the next day and loaded up our minivan. Problem solved.

We then had a much bigger problem.

We needed a strainer, and when I say strainer, I don't mean the kind you have in your kitchen for pasta. The strainer had to separate hundreds of gallons of water, sugar, and whey from the casein protein mass quickly. It's what makes Greek yogurt so thick and protein-dense. Most Greek yogurt facilities used a massive centrifuge machine that costs $500,000. We found a rickety old one for $150,000. We hadn't sold one bottle yet, though. How the heck were we going to cash in our kids' college fund to invest in equipment? It was too risky. A speed bump.

Stuff happens all the time while you are climbing. You lay out your strategic plan before you hit the mountain—where you'll camp, the route, and other details—and then you run into unplanned events thanks to Mother Nature. This happened on our second attempt on Mount Rainier back in 2002. (I had already summited once before after two weather-related unsuccessful attempts.)

We planned to stay at Camp Muir the first night and have an easy push to high camp on the Ingraham Flats on day two, requiring only a few hours of climbing. The previous year we pushed all the way to the Flats on day one. It knocked the piss out of this fifty-two-year-old man.

The second year, everything was lining up: the spectacular weather, great plan of attack, and rested bodies, and then we got word that there was a huge cornice overhanging on the trail. I love the Avalanche. org definition of a cornice: "Cornices are the fatal attraction of the mountains, their beauty matched only by their danger." It's an over-hanging slab of ice and snow that looks like a wave created by winds sweeping up the snow and depositing it on the ridge. The one on our mountain was no ordinary cornice. The rangers reported that it looked like a fifty-foot tidal wave, making it potentially lethal to come near. Blocked again!

The team reviewed our plan and laid out our options. We could approach the cornice, trek down the mountain for an hour, and then climb back up another two hours, or we could abandon our summit attempt. I hated the idea of adding three unnecessary, tiring hours of climbing to our twelve-hour plan. The alternatives were turning back again or risking death. The guides and climbers discussed the situation and options. The long, tiring route it was, and as a team, we summited together safely.

To address our straining situation at B'more Organic, I huddled our team together—Dr. Lee, Jennifer, Noah, and the Pitango workers. We needed something inexpensive, safe, and clean to strain our skyr until we had proof of concept that the crazy idea I had in our kitchen was going to come to fruition. We needed to know that people would actually pay for a bottle.

Dr. Lee suggested we buy six brand new plastic garbage cans and six industrial strainers—jumbo-sized variations of what you have in your kitchen. We would line them with cheesecloth, pour in the yogurt, and then let it sit overnight in the commercial walk-in cooler. We all agreed, and we reached the "summit" together. It worked!

We produced our skyr and bottled it. It tasted much better than we expected. The live version was even better than what we had produced in the lab. We didn't expect that bonus.

And people bought it.

A bottle of B'more Organic. People bought it!

"I hate yogurt."

I was trying to help Andy where I could. It was hard to get behind a product that ruined my appetite, but my kids loved it, so call me a non-active investor. We never had fewer than twelve bottles in our refrigerator.

Whenever my girlfriend (who is now my wife) and I went to a friend's house for dinner we took a few bottles with us and asked them to taste it. Everyone seemed to like it a lot, and most said they would buy it if they saw it in a store.

—Eric Kronthal

Why B'More Organic?

After my flag-carrying experience, I knew that with B'more Organic, everything started with our mission: to take a bite out of disease. We did it by making an extremely healthy product. It started with the highest quality, healthy, organic, grass-fed milk we could find. The smoothies were going be high in protein, have no added sugar, be one hundred percent organic, be GMO-free, be gluten-free, and contain probiotics. Those things would help Americans prevent disease. To help the millions of people around the world affected by the diseases of MS and breast cancer, we donated one percent of sales to Jodi's Climb for Hope. We felt that every bottle sold helped reduce heart disease and diabetes and slowed the advancement of cancer that fed on sugar. Each sale also benefited disease research.

I was privileged enough to know some good people. Our neighbors owned a string of five yoga studios called Charm City Yoga. A high school friend owned five great running stores—Charm City Run—and there were Chris Warner's three climbing gyms. These people were all kind enough to sell our smoothies at their locations. The climbers at Chris's Earth Treks gym loved it. I found myself driving forty minutes each way to Rockville after a long day of work to continually refill beverage refrigerators or going to the gym in Timonium early on Sunday mornings. On other nights and weekends, I handed out samples at those stores to promote the new product. Naturally Jennifer wasn't pleased with me working around the clock. I had a day job and worked nights and weekends building B'more Organic.

We had found a way around investing in the centrifuge, and now we found a workaround for not having a labeling machine. We put all the labels on by hand, which meant putting a label on every bottle and then delivering bottles to the locations. It was a lot of work.

After a little while I got up the nerve to approach some supermarkets. My friend Greg Strott, who was with us in Iceland and worked in the beverage distribution business, offered to hold my hand and take me to a few independent stores.

We walked into the locally owned Roots Market in Clarksville, Maryland, without an appointment. The company had two locations. The nice CFO let us meet with him unannounced. We put the bottles on his desk, and I launched into my sales pitch: "We're local, we're organic, we give one percent of sales to MS and breast cancer re-search here at Johns Hopkins. Wanna try some?"

He replied, "Okay, we'll take it."

I prepared to rebut him. Did he just say we're in?

"But don't you want to try it first?" I asked.

"No, you're local, you're organic, and you give money to a local char-ity. We'll take 'em. And we'll pay you cash on delivery."

Wait, what? I've worked in sales all my life. I sold advertising for twenty years. Selling is hard. There's wrestling over price, terms, and when the contract will start. This conversation was a joke. I'd never walked into a cold sales call and walked out ten minutes later with a contract better than I asked for.

Full of confidence, Greg and I drove to another locally owned health food store, David's Naturals. It had three locations.

Same drill. Same result.

Uh oh. Now we had to produce them in Lancaster, get them down to

Baltimore, store them, and put labels on them.

Jen and I bought a second refrigerator, put it in the basement, and kept the smoothies down there. There's nothing like making eight trips up and down basement stairs to make you feel successful.

"This tangent happens"

Here is a normal guy dealing with the struggles of the family business and the tragedy of his sister. He exposes himself to a new and uncomfortable situation and takes a risk with Jodi's Climb for Hope. The group is fired up and has amazing success down in Ecuador. Andy and the group give it the next tidbit of energy, go up to Kilimanjaro and get the next bit of energy. Then they are off in Iceland, and all of a sudden a tangent happens that nobody would have ever expected, and Andy's an entrepreneur.

—Chris Warner
Mountaineer, leadership educator, and entrepreneur

Our mission resonated with people. We received phone calls and emails about how we changed people's lives. Some had gotten stomach surgery and needed our smoothies because they needed protein-dense food without sugar. Others gave it to loved ones who were battling cancer and needed nourishment.

Kathleen Overman ran our experiential marketing. Her aunt was suffering a long, slow death, often not eating. Kathleen brought a steady supply of B'more Organic, usually the only thing her aunt could stomach that provided nutrition.

Often when we were having a bad day, we'd get an email reminding us why we worked so hard.

Hi,

I just wanted to let you know how happy and pleased I am to have discovered your Skyr.

I fell ill in the summer and was hospitalized, ended up losing all my muscle mass, and wrecked my gut health. Since I've started drinking your product I've noticed a big difference. I've gained muscle back and feel great! —Teresa

Hello Andrew,

My name is Mare and I'm from Birmingham, Alabama. I am currently a junior at Auburn University, studying accounting. I discovered your wonderful product just a few days ago while I was serving as a camp counselor at an overnight camp. Our only food options were cafeteria food, and due to a wheat allergy and a strong aversion to overly processed foods, all I found myself eating on a day-to-day basis was salad and an enormous amount of carrots. And while carrots are a wonderful dietary option, they don't constitute a substantial meal.

All of this to say that I needed substance, and I wasn't getting it. There was a Publix somewhat nearby the camp, and one day when I had to drive off campus, I was feeling particularly undernourished, but being on a time crunch, couldn't get anything particularly substantial. I swung by Publix hoping to find some sort of probiotic drink to give me a quick protein boost. I spotted B'more, took a peek at the nutritional facts, compared them to a few other brands, and was absolutely blown away. The sugar content was significantly lower, while the amount of protein was significantly higher. I purchased it without a second thought, unconcerned about what it would taste like, but on my first sip, I was once again blown away. It was smooth, light, had a delicious strawberry taste, but was not overly sweet or abrasively sour.

I fell in love. I've consumed a lot of yogurt in my life, and your probiotic drink is the best one I've ever had. You have a new fan and lifetime committed customer. Thanks for making such a great product that's wholesome, healthy, hearty, delicious, and nutritious.

I've never contacted a company about a product before, but I couldn't go without telling you how much I appreciate and enjoy what you've made. Keep up the great work!

All the best
Mare

Everyone knew our mission—all our employees, including our interns; our suppliers; our retail buyers; and naturally our end users—our customers. Everyone worked harder to reach that mission. We wrote our mission on our bottle, our website, and social media pages. Every few months we'd make a post reminding people why we were in business. We posted it on the walls and included it in every new intern's training.

Every communication with our retail customers—the men and women who chose to include our product in their stores—referred to it. I had the privilege of meeting with Tom Crowder, the lead dairy buyer for *all* of Kroger's 2,400 stores, a very important and powerful man. He knew our mission. He emailed me every August: "Hey Andy, letting you know I'm leaving for my annual MS 150 Ride tomorrow; thinking of your wife." The most powerful man in our category in the country emailed me about his role in taking a bite out of disease.

He knew our mission because I repeated it over and over. I was sick of saying it, but others were not. In most emails to customers, retail buyers, or suppliers I'd thank them with, "Because of you we're getting closer to our mission of taking a bite out of disease."

A mission is different from a vision. A vision is where you're going to be or what you're going to accomplish in three to five years. For example, at B'more Organic, the vision was to change the way the world ate in five years.

Well, the world definitely changed the way it ate in that time frame. Was it because of us? Of course! Hard to say, but in those five years, Americans added better sources of protein to their diets, and companies added more no-sugar-added options, so we believe we were part of the original ripple that caused that major wave. We accomplished our vision.

A mission is like a purpose. It's the reason a person or an organization exists.

Everyone wants to serve a purpose. Jennifer's purpose is to raise healthy, stable children. People don't get out of bed on cold, dark mornings for just a paycheck. They get out of bed to serve a purpose.

The flags we were carrying at B'more Organic were to help take a bite out of disease. It is not only why our operations manager, Amanda Sains, got out of bed; it's why she worked late into the night. Amanda, whose mother had recently been diagnosed with lung cancer, bought into our mission. She lived our mission. When we mistakenly ran out of bottles, Amanda worked twelve-hour days to find a new source. When we launched in Costco, she worked three straight weeks without taking a day off.

"Amanda, it's 10:30 at night. Please stop texting me," was a usual message I'd have to send back to the twenty-eight-year-old millennial. At other times she'd be answering Facebook messages from customers at ten at night as if she were living in another time zone or was working the second shift.

We all love those jokes about millennials getting trophies for showing up, giving them a false sense of entitlement. The joke is on us, the Gen-Xers and baby boomers. What we got wrong was that millennials aren't looking for a just a paycheck; they're looking to serve a purpose. I love our millennials. B'more Organic gave its millennial employees a sense of purpose, and they gave unstoppable effort. It wasn't just Amanda. Our operations people, Tom Barnes and Sarah Frisch, were the same way. The interns were too.

When starting a business, a nonprofit, or a marriage, you have to start with your agreed-upon purpose, though Jennifer didn't like that I chose to talk about it on our honeymoon. In the case of my marriage, I stole the best purpose ever, written by my friend, Mark Jankowski, who's an author, speaker, and coach. "To be the bridge upon which our children walk." I love it! Marriages exist before kids; the kids need support for a long time, and then once again you're alone with your spouse.

Obviously purpose statements are essential for businesses as well. Why did someone need another yogurt? Because ours was designed to take a bite out of disease.

Shared Passion

I met Andy at the Natural Products Trade Show. He was working at the B'more Organic booth, and I was working on a new loyalty program for natural-products consumers called EcoBonus. The natural-products industry runs on relationships and shared passion, and since I really liked Andy's product and his mission, I thought we were a perfect match. Sure enough, Andy became one of our first clients.

—Tiger Beaudoin
Entrepreneur and Jodi's Climb for Hope volunteer

GET COMFORTABLE
BEING UNCOMFORTABLE

"Adventure without risk is Disneyland"

—**Douglas Coupland**, *Generation-X*

Jennifer's passion for Ethiopia began in middle school. In her words:

I had always dreamed of joining the Peace Corps and serving in Ethiopia. I've had an obsession with Ethiopia since I wrote a report on it when I was twelve, and I never lost my love for the place. When I mentioned the idea to my parents, they said, "We're not going to lose you to Ethiopia; you can't go." When Andy and I decided to adopt, Andy was in Israel at a time when thousands of Jewish refugees from Ethiopia were immigrating to Israel. He met some of the Ethiopian children, and they made Sabbath candle holders for him as a gift. We started using those for our Friday night Shabbat candles. When it came down to deciding where to adopt from, we looked at each other and said, "Ethiopia, right?"

Ethiopia is a country of 115 million people, about one-third of the United States' population. They have 4.5 million orphans. That staggering five percent rate stems from the ravages of the long-term AIDS epidemic and extreme poverty. The latter issue is exacerbated by drought and political corruption. In fact, Ethiopia is the eighteenth-poorest country in the world, with an average gross national income of $1,590 per person, a big $60 higher than Haiti.

Caught up in all of this were two beautiful babies born in the late spring of 2010 in Bahir Dar, a large city in the northern region. It sits on the shores of Lake Tana. Before the rainy season the babies were brought down to the capital, Addis Ababa. It's a bustling city of more than three million residents.

When the rainy season ended, Jennifer and I jumped on a plane to meet the babies and legally adopt them. We wanted to start in Bahir Dar to get a sense of where our babies came from. The poverty overwhelmed us. In Bahir Dar we saw six-year-old boys walking a mile one way to fetch five gallons of water from the Blue Nile. They carried the buckets back on their heads. A gallon of water weighs eight pounds. "Houses" made out of tin were ten feet by ten feet.

I don't know if it's genetics or poverty, but Ethiopians are the nicest people in the world. A waitress at our hotel invited us back to her home in Bahir Dar. We made our way out there and sat in her living room. A small TV mounted to the wall aired local music. I, with my low emotional quotient, asked where the bedroom was for the five of them. (Her sister had died of AIDS.) She pulled back a curtain revealing a one-hundred-square-foot room sporting a queen-sized bed.

"Here," the hostess told us.

She then showed us outside where a teepee-like skeletal structure stood made with tree branches. Inside smoldered a fire where women came daily to bake the traditional *injera*, flatbread made from teff flour.

We flew south to Addis Ababa to finally meet our new children.

Eskedar, a girl born on May 21, was small with tightly braided hair. Eskedar means "a long way" in Amharic, the main Ethiopian language. Her name would certainly ring true for her. She'd come a long way in her near future. It didn't take us long to give her an American name: Joss Eskedar. It's Jewish tradition to name children after loved ones who have died, often using just the first letter. The letter "J" was used for Joss in memory of Jodi, whose death left a huge hole in all of us. We turned our pain into passion. We received the best gift in the world.

Eighteen days after Joss, a huge baby boy was born and given the name Muluken, meaning "a full day." Ethiopians love hearing that name because it's shared with a famous Ethiopian musician. It's like walking around with a son named Bono.

We didn't take Jodi's advice after all, to name the boy Ethan. Many years before Jodi died, she told me that she was not going to use the name Brona because she wanted me to have that opportunity. Jodi gave birth three weeks after my father died. She named the baby Charles Alter Buerger Augustini. Her two other children are Caroline and Max. We named our son Bronsten Muluken, after my birth mother, Brona.

People told us all the time what a great thing we did to adopt children from Ethiopia. Jennifer and I never saw it that way. We get far more from it than the two children do. Joss and Bronsten fulfill Jennifer's mission in life. They are her two flags. She fights through horrible MS

Jen, Andy, Joss, Bronsten, and Mt Shasta

pain to play football with them, even if it means not being able to get out of bed the next day. Every day, Jennifer crawls out of bed and fights through fatigue to play games, do crafts, or assist the children with homework. Nothing's going to stop her from getting those flags to the summit.

A Mountaineer Who Hates the Cold

I knew in my early twenties that I wanted to run my own business, so my friend and mentor, B Boykin, encouraged me to get an MBA. I figured that if it's something I had to do, I might as well enjoy the time. I applied and got into the University of Colorado. I left for Boulder in the summer of 1991, and school was a blast. There were many like-minded people who were looking to learn and looking for adventures.

In the summer of 1992, before our second year of graduate school, Drew Esson asked me if I would join him and Rob Siegal on a hike. I loved hiking, of course. We were going to hike Grays and Torreys. I hiked much over the years, but I had never hiked a 14,000-foot mountain. What was the big deal? Hour after hour, the hike seemed to go on forever. I was exhausted, and then came the scree section— small rocks that made me feel that I was walking on BBs up a steep hill, with a pack on, at 13,000 feet. Just when that challenge got to be enough, the thin air started to affect me.

I had never hiked that high before, experiencing the light-headedness, swollen fingers, or shortness of breath. After countless hours I crested the summit and took in the amazing view. After minutes of rest, Rob and Drew descended and were heading for the Grays summit. I thought, *The view can't be much different than this. Why would I want to go up another hill?*

But I was hooked. Who knew that climbing all of Colorado's fifty-four 14,000-foot peaks was a thing? Two down. I managed to check off five more, including Mount Elbert, the highest in Colorado at 14,439 feet and the second tallest in the continental United States. Only forty-seven left to go!

Between the outdoor pursuits we took courses in accounting and learned how to read an income statement and a balance sheet. I took courses in finance and learned how to value companies from a mergers and acquisitions perspective. I took marketing courses, communications classes, and even strategy courses. I learned a lot in the classroom and from working in groups. I gained many skills on how to run a business.

I graduated with an MBA in finance in 1993. Similar to my climbing, I took classes and understood finance, but I was no expert in finance.

I much preferred marketing.

All those courses, outdoor experiences, and help from my friends stuck with me and stuck in me. I pursue business ventures and outdoor adventures—the bedrock for my work and personal life.

More than a decade later, one of my mountaineering expeditions included a winter ascent up Mount Whitney. I was a bit older at that point with a wife, two kids, a dog, and a busy day job, which left me little time to train properly. We carried heavy packs on day one and made a low camp. We pushed even higher on day two and set up a camp four thousand feet below the summit.

I never sleep well in tents, and sleeping at ten thousand feet makes it even harder. The thinner air makes breathing more challenging. I'm prone to getting Cheyne Stokes syndrome. It's similar to sleep apnea and gets triggered in me when sleeping above ten thousand feet. When you sleep, your brain tells your heart to slow down and relax; you don't need as much oxygen. At higher altitudes, however, there is less oxygen in the atmosphere. Your heart has to work harder to pump more blood, because the air contains less oxygen so the blood does too. When I fall asleep, I wake up gasping for breath. It's an off-putting feeling to wake up every fifteen minutes or so feeling as though you're suffocating. One time on Chimborazo (elevation 20,564 feet) in Ecuador I slept at sixteen thousand feet for a few days. I had to trick my brain into thinking that I wasn't sleeping, so I "slept" sitting up.

Add on top of my having difficulty breathing, the tent flapped in the thirty-mile-an-hour winds, my tent mates snored, and I had to crawl over them and out of the tent into the freezing cold to pee. I didn't sleep much for two straight nights. Then there was a five a.m. start. I was more tired than normal. The altitude adds another difficult element. There wasn't much snow that winter, so there was a lot of loose rock uncovered. Sometimes I'd walk two feet forward and slide back one. It was tiring with little oxygen and frustrating emotionally. I spent a great deal of energy on the ascent, more than I normally do. I got a little light-headed and even nauseated and thought I'd puke at one point. I pushed on, as I always did.

The number-one rule of mountaineering: getting to the top is optional, but getting back down is mandatory. On my two Nalgene water bottles, I'd write the names of each of my children, Joss and Bronsten, so every sip of water I'd take, I'd be reminded to come back home—alive.

Tiger, Danny Kaplan, and I made up the base group for the climbs for a few years and recruited others to join. The three of us got very close, and those two pushed me a lot, not only in the mountains, but with our nonprofit, to make it bigger, better, and raise more money for charity. Danny and Tiger both were touched deeply by cancer and also felt the power of what Jodi's Climb for Hope was doing. Every year we sobbed on the summits together, remembering those we'd lost and appreciating the loved ones who overcame cancer.

We all made it to the summit, and celebrated at the highest point in the Continental United States (14,500 feet). We then hydrated, got some food down, and took photos before going down. The long, brutal descent made my thighs burn; my knees ached. My toes banged the front of my boots. I was so tired that I didn't recognize the area where we were on the way down to camp. Danny kept telling me that we were getting close, and then an hour would go by and we still weren't back at camp. Danny said we were getting closer. This communication was repeated for several more hours. My gas tank was empty. I had nothing else after thirteen hours on the mountain. I felt like just stopping there, about one final hour before camp.

I didn't.

I kept putting one foot in front of the other. I chose not to lie down. I chose to continue, pushing through the pain. Lying down and dying on a mountain isn't an option. I looked at "Joss" and "Bronsten" when I took a drink. They needed their father, and human nature doesn't like you dying. You keep going. The human body has an amazing capacity to do far more than you think. We're hard-wired not to push too far so we don't overdo it, but we still can go on. Our minds tell us to stop, but our bodies can go far further if you override what your mind is telling you. As my climbing guide, Ricky Haro from Rare Earth Adventures reminds us, "Your body is an avatar; your mind just has to tell it what to do. It's about slow, relentless forward progress."

I overrode that extreme fatigue my body was telling my brain. "Lie down and die," my body said. My brain told my body to keep putting one foot in front of the other.

We arrived in camp right before dark.

Teach Yourself Not to Quit

In that outdoor classroom of life I got the best lesson and preparation for being an entrepreneur. Business school teaches you about the time value of money and how to deliver feedback to employees. It teaches you accounting, finance, and marketing, all the essentials to understand how a business functions. Yes, it helps to read a balance sheet and understand cash flow, but what you can't or don't learn in business school is how to be comfortable with being uncomfortable—how to overcome mental and physical limits and go far further than you think you can. Business school doesn't teach you what to do when your business is out of cash and payroll is due in forty-eight hours or what to do when you can pay your main supplier but not yourself—the mortgage or food for your wife and, in my case, two babies.

The training I've received mountaineering—being uncomfortable—provided me with my best preparation. I hate cold. I mean I hate it. (I tell people maybe it's because I have too little body fat.) I get cold so easily that I have to eat dinners in my tent in my sleeping bag that's rated to zero degrees.

My wife and I love watching those SEAL Team TV shows, the kind showing the training they go through. We watched one where they are in the cold ocean water for hours. In the dark. In the middle of the night. They're cold, hungry, scared, thirsty, and tired. They're getting water up their noses. They finally get out of the water and roll in the sand, getting fine grains in places we couldn't imagine. Why? To get comfortable being uncomfortable.

It's easier to quit, tap out, when I'm sick of the stress of it all. Sick of sleeping like a baby at night—which means waking up at two a.m., four a.m., and six a.m. crying—worried that when I get to work, suppliers will threaten to cut me off or that my plant just called and our product tested too high for yeast and we can't make the first delivery we promised to a new, large account.

There are many days you just want to quit. No business school teaches you not to. In fact, sometimes they teach you the opposite—when you have negative equity, you're out of business. Game over. You have to seek opportunities to teach yourself not to quit.

I've discovered many other methods to learn to get comfortable being uncomfortable other than joining the SEALs. In best-selling author Tim Ferriss's notorious book, *The Four Hour Work Week* he tells would-be entrepreneurs how to learn to be uncomfortable without having to climb a mountain or run a marathon.

He suggests (pre-COVID-19) going to a Starbucks and lying down on the floor for ten seconds or when ordering coffee always ask for a 10 percent discount. There are many other ways than having to climb a mountain or running your first marathon. I've tried other methods as well that have less risk and added health benefits, for example taking a two-minute cold shower or a three-day water-only fast.

Getting comfortable being uncomfortable is important in many aspects of my life as a climber, businessperson, and father.

Shortly after I started B'more Organic, another guy in our area started another drinkable yogurt company. That guy had access to a lot of capital, actual experience in the food and beverage industry, unlike me, and was in the same selling region I was in. We were going to compete for the same shelf space in the same local retailers to get started. That guy was going to kick my butt.

It was a tough slog for both of us. Most yogurts at the time were in cups and required a spoon. Despite drinkable yogurt being popular in Europe, Americans thought it strange. It was an educational process for retail buyers and end consumers. Getting drinking yogurt in stores was hand-to-hand combat. I had to summon my inner Navy SEAL. I had to be a tired mountaineer finding basecamp after eighteen hours on the mountain.

After a few years the other guy quit. He tapped out. It was too hard. Little did he know that drinkable yogurt was the next hot food trend after the Greek yogurt craze. B'more Organic rode that trend and became the fifth fastest-growing natural/organic food brand in the U.S. in 2017, according to *Inc.* magazine. If we had quit, we would have missed out completely. As Wayne Gretzky famously said, "You miss 100 percent of the shots you don't take." The challenge is to fight the pain, the discomfort. You fight through the dark moments, the days you have to fight to not pull the covers over your head and go back to sleep.

In the mountains, I learned a lot about fighting through discomfort.

What is Success?

The story of the climbing of a mountain is there only to make a point of the overall journey. The climb is not the center of the story. Yes, people go to an amazing setting. Yes, they have a life-enriching experience. Yes, they summit the peak. But an expedition is not a success when they reach the summit. It's a success when they go back home and apply what they learned on the mountain to normal life; when the experience makes them better. Look at how climbing changed Andy's life and what he learned about himself. He found skyr yogurt and became an entrepreneur.

—Chris Warner
Mountaineer, leadership educator, and entrepreneur

GO FAST AND LIGHT

"If you are not embarrassed by the first version of
your product, you've launched too late."

—Reid Hoffman, founder of LinkedIn

There are amazing times on a mountain when you can stop and appreciate the experience, the beauty, and the journey and snap a few pictures. My buddy Tiger does this to the extreme, getting his camera out at two a.m. and stopping the entire rope team for precious minutes in subfreezing temperatures. Frequently! (We do have some great photos and video to show for those annoying moments, though.)

Then there are times on the mountain that you simply have to go fast and light. People talk about the death zone on Everest—the area above 26,000 feet where there's not enough oxygen for anything to survive, not even bacteria, for an extended period. That's why dead bodies remain there decades later; they don't decompose. Many climbers choose to use bottled oxygen to extend the time they can spend in the death zone. Regardless, you don't want to be there long. Go fast and light.

Even on the much smaller mountains that I experienced, challenges remain. Weather can kill a climber at much lower elevations. You have to be super strict on rest stops: ten minutes, ensure food and water consumption, stop only once per sixty minutes. Keep moving the entire time during that hour. Go fast.

Sometimes you discover weather coming in—high winds, dropping temperatures, snow, and very low visibility, all conditions that often result in death. You have only a small window to go for the summit and return *safely* before some storm hits.

Avoiding death is normally the goal for most mountaineers.

The other issue to deal with later in the day is melting snow. Climbing is more difficult in slush and more lethal. On some mountains, such as Mount Rainier, the 14,410-foot high volcano that spans five rivers, you have to cross snow bridges to get to the summit. If you leave too late, by the time you reach the summit and descend, on your way down the bridges can collapse under your weight. You don't need to be a mountain climber to understand that you don't want to fall into a seemingly bottomless crevasse.

It's not just weather that can kill you. There are dangerous sections where you don't want to linger. On Mount Rainier there's a section just above Camp Muir and before Ingraham Flats at 10,200 feet where rocks roll down the mountain above you. Some are the size of a VW Beetle. If one hits you, game over. The boulder doesn't discriminate based on who's an experienced climber. It's a luck-of-the-draw thing. If a huge rock hits you, you're dead, along with the others on your rope team. Again, moving fast and light through this section is highly encouraged to avoid instant death. The less time you spend in this exposed section, the better chance you have of going home to see your family again. Every time, we have to remind Tiger to keep his camera in his pocket. No photos. His wife and kids love him too much.

To go fast, you have to go light. We keep the packs to the bare safe minimum. (At the other extreme, you still want to ensure you have all the gear needed in case of emergency—down jacket, foul-weather gear, food, water, and first aid kit.) We pull out unnecessary items. We cut our toothbrushes in half to save ounces; one pair of underwear, one T-shirt. For me it sadly means no French press coffeemaker and no pound of freshly ground organic fair-trade Ethiopian coffee. I had to suffer through Starbucks instant coffee. Yuck.

Fast and Light at B'more Organic

I'm no visionary like Steve Jobs. I just saw the protein and anti-sugar trends coming. I was introduced to Joe Dillon, a speaker at a Vistage group, a CEO roundtable. I remember the date. We all recall important dates in our lives. I vividly remember December 4, 1998.

Joe quoted an old Buddhist saying, "When the student is ready, the teacher will appear." I was a ready student.

My father died at age fifty-eight undergoing his *second* heart bypass surgery. Twenty pounds overweight in my then-current state, I had been taking statin drugs to reduce my cholesterol since I was twenty-five years old, and I was sick and tired of being sick and tired. I was so fatigued I refused to take part in meetings after lunch.

Joe taught us how to eat right and exercise. Remember, this was 1998, when you could allegedly eat as many SnackWell's fat-free cookies as you wanted and not get fat (*wrong!*) because we believed that fat made us fat. We believed that cholesterol from egg yolks gave us heart disease. We thought orange juice was a great way to start our day because it had vitamin C. (*Wrong!*)

Never mind that essential fats are critical for body function and create a satiated feeling to turn off our hunger. Never mind that we get heart disease from inflammation largely caused by eating too much sugar and refined carbohydrates.

I, along with the majority of Americans, consumed all the wrong stuff and avoided all the right stuff. We thought fat was bad, staying away from raw nuts/seeds, avocado, and olive oil. That's why America is the wealthiest nation in the history of the world and the most overweight. Almost half of our country is obese, not just overweight, but dangerously obese. One half. At the same time, despite our wealth, we're malnourished because we're not consuming enough good food to get things like essential fats or nutrients. Joe taught me that according to the CDC, 87 percent of diseases are preventable with lifestyle changes—stop smoking, eat right, and exercise.

I thought his advice was a bit looney, but I gave it a try. The weight melted off, I had much more energy, and my cholesterol dropped to 185 without statin drugs. I became a nut for this lifestyle. I drove people crazy because that's all I talked about, and I lectured people who weren't eating correctly. I annoyed the hell out of people with my preaching.

It began to build inside of me over the next few years. I realized my calling in life: to help people get healthier by helping them prevent disease. I even resigned from the University of Maryland Cancer Center Advisory Board because our efforts were around raising money to cure cancer. I needed to focus my energy on prevention, and then my sister got a disease, a very bad disease, stage four metastatic cancer.

Suddenly I became interested in fundraising for breast cancer treatments again.

I also had B'more Organic. We had created the first organic protein smoothie with no added sugar. We used organic stevia, a centuries-old herb used in South America. It's the only sweetener that's organic, has no calories, and has no effect on blood sugar. All the other junk out there is either toxic, spikes your blood sugar, and/or has calories.

We had Dr. Frank Lee on board, and we were moving fast. He'd whip up samples in his lab at the University of Vermont. He'd then overnight the test samples. We'd try them and give them to friends for input.

My wife has many gifts and talents. I'm not sure if it's a blessing or curse or both, but she has an immensely discerning palate. She's not a wine drinker, but when she tries it, she tells me what notes she's experiencing, while I need to read the back of the bottle to learn about what flavors I'm supposed to experience. She nails it every time. Her sense of smell is strong, maybe a little too strong. We joke that she can smell the neighbors cooking bacon a hundred feet away.

The samples arrived and Jennifer would rip them apart. "Too tart."

Two weeks later, she'd comment, "Too chalky."

The next batch: "Not enough mango."

After about six weeks I had enough. I saw the storm coming in the distance. I figuratively looked at the barometric pressure on my climbing watch. It was dropping. We needed to move fast and light.

"Let's go, Jennifer!" It was like climbing with Tiger. We had to put the cameras away and move. "It's not perfect, and we'll fix it when it's out," I told her as she scowled at me.

Greek yogurt was exploding. Skyr is very similar to Greek yogurt. I could see Americans craving protein, and people finally woke up to the fact that sugar was literally killing them. It was a matter of time before companies would make a drinkable Greek yogurt with no added sugar. As the little guys, we needed a head start before the storm rolled in.

Reid Hoffman, the founder of LinkedIn, once remarked, "If you are not embarrassed by the first version of your product, you've launched too late."

I wasn't embarrassed by our first version of B'More Organic, as Reid Hoffman would have wanted, and I wasn't 100 percent proud either. Still, the feedback from Krony's then-girlfriend, Stacie, was pretty positive. She created a focus group with her friends at work—typical customers. They were mostly educated women. We had a chance every single week to tweak the product, add a dash more stevia, dial back on the fruit, take the pH up a hair.

That's the extent of focus grouping we did. Like the old Henry Ford saying, "If we'd asked people what they wanted, they would have said a faster horse."

We limited our focus group to friends. We knew where the world was moving. In 1998 no one was asking for an iPhone yet, but that's where the world was heading, so we didn't spend a lot of time and money researching our future.

Our ten-minute rest break was over. I heard Lieutenant Dan shouting at us on Cotopaxi to "Get those packs on, and let's go. This is taking too long!"

So we got going. We hit the shelves on August 1, 2010, ten months after the idea popped into my head.

Surprisingly, people loved it.

B'more Organic's Summit

We were light. We kept things small and light. We didn't have a lot of money to spend, so we used guerilla marketing, a lean staff, and liberal use of brilliant interns making $15 an hour. These kids worked hard because they believed in us. Being light enabled us to move quickly as if we were roped up and avoiding crevasses together.

We had placement in only a few climbing gyms, running stores, and local natural stores. Our friend Michele Tsucalas, the brilliant founder of Michele's Granola, encouraged us to get a booth at the Natural Products Expo East, the Super Bowl of the natural foods industry. It took place in Baltimore every year, so there was no need for flights, hotels, or transporting the product. We scraped together $5,000 to make it happen. While it was a huge amount of money for our tiny business, if we had to go somewhere else, we would have had to spend $10,000 more.

I made my way through the most dazzling displays of the coolest brands. Honest Tea. Dr. Bronner's. Stonyfield's Organic Yogurt. I felt as if I was walking through an NFL locker room, up close and personal with all my favorite superstars.

I wandered through the crowded floor toward our booth. I worried that at this Super Bowl our booth would look more like a high school football team. There it was. Standing behind the table was a beautiful redhead. She looked like one of the models who gets hired to work auto shows. She sported a B'more Organic T-shirt. That model was my wife and co-founder, and our booth looked terrific. With no money, Jennifer had done a great job to make us look like a real company. Simple fruit displays and the nicely merchandised table had the perfect family-owned look.

Jennifer has an IQ approaching the Mensa level. She's the world's best mom. She's a sought-after psychotherapist by day. Business is not her strength, yet there she was, managing our investment, in charge most of the day.

"Along came thousands of people to try our product"

Our first sales spike came when we stumbled onto the Natural Products Expo East trade show. We didn't even understand the industry enough to know what a big deal it was to go to Expo East when we signed up. We were rookies and had no idea what we were doing. We just got a booth, made a poster, and put out some fresh fruit and our smoothies, and then along came thousands of people wanting to try our product. My role was figuring out which of those people could help us and introducing them to Andy.

—Jennifer Buerger

I gave her a huge, huge bear hug.

"How was your day, sweetheart?" I asked with the greatest of anticipation.

"Well," Jennifer started in her natural voice, which is shockingly high pitched for her athletic body, "someone came by from United something. Maybe United Foods. They want to distribute our products."

"You mean U-N-F-I?!" I screamed. United Foods Inc., or UNFI, was just The Distributor for natural products. Its footprint can give you national distribution overnight.

"Yeah, I think that's it." She demurred. "Oh, and Wegmans came by and wants to carry us."

In thirty minutes, my world changed. The little product we whipped up in our kitchen was going to be in the Hunt Valley Wegmans store near our house. Excitement!

A few weeks later we heard that B'more Organic wasn't going to be in just one Wegmans; we were being placed in fifty of its eighty stores. By keeping our eyes off our feet and looking ahead, we found the best route up the mountain. What a huge moment in our lives! As my friend Alissa Sears says about her communications firm, "We take you from dream to mainstream." It felt like a dream.

As was our custom, we celebrated briefly and got back to work. The problem was that our plant was at capacity. It took us months, and we found another facility. As soon as we moved, I hit the streets again.

I walked down to that same Whole Foods we were buying skyr from and showed them our product. The guy looked it over. "Organic, local, and no prohibited ingredients. I'll take it to our regional director."

We held our breath.

A few weeks later we received the email. We were accepted in

Andy and Millennial Marketing Machine, Amanda Sains: "We were accepted at Whole Foods!"

Whole Foods. I'm still at a loss for words for what the news meant to us, not just as a business, but as a guy who had a silly dream for years and was finally tenacious enough to go for it. I'll die knowing we placed a product in my favorite retail store. Again, it's like climbing a mountain. You celebrate this accomplishment, and you still have work to do, like getting back down.

We celebrated and went back to work.

Not long after we successfully launched in those retailers, I received an email from a distant acquaintance, David Schleider. He wanted to meet. As the head of an organization, I got untold sales solicitations. It was impossible to keep up. I couldn't figure out what David wanted. Our fathers were friends and we had many friends in common. I've tried to always get a nugget out of all my commitments no matter how painful. I was sure he would give me a nugget, or at least, a free cup of coffee. I could handle his sales pitch.

We met at a coffee shop near my house. David had founded a company based on a process that made a much truer lemon drink experience in a sugar-like packet. It was called True Lemon. He grew the company exponentially and diversified into other citrus flavors and eventually naturally flavored drink powders.

Over a hot coffee David threw out business suggestions for me: "You should add something to mask the stevia flavor; you should stick to being a regional brand…"

What the heck did this guy want from me?

It wasn't until the bottom of my free coffee that it dawned on me why he wanted to meet. He just wanted to help me. Who does that? As we wrapped up, he threw out one more suggestion: "You should meet Frank Rich. He's our broker."

In the media business, people were hyper-competitive. No one wanted to help. All of a sudden people were reaching out to help me.

Within two weeks Frank called and wanted to take Jennifer and me out to lunch in Baltimore's Little Italy. I was still wary of people trying to sell me stuff. I'm horrible at saying no, but we were starving entrepreneurs, so it was a rare chance to take my wife out for a nice meal.

Frank's son, Frankie, tossed a pitch book on the table and went over every page in excruciating detail about how the company had grown True Citrus and could do the same for us. My eyes glazed over and I tuned out. We weren't ready for those guys yet. Thanks for the great meal, guys.

A few weeks later Frank called. "Hey, if I could get you a meeting with Kroger, would you want that?"

Hey, if I could fly to the moon, would I want to go? Sure, why not, right?

"Andrew and Jennifer are delightful."

First of all, I liked the product. It was a healthy drink, on trend, and had a good point of entry into the marketplace in the dairy category. Andrew and Jennifer are delightful, and learning about their backgrounds, including the deaths of Andrew's father and sister, and their commitment to fighting cancer, cemented my interest in working with them.

—Frank Rich

Kroger was one of the top five largest grocery chains in the country with more than 2,400 stores covering much of the United States, including Alaska. No way was Kroger going to meet with us. We were nobody; nobody with a crazy dream.

Frank got us the meeting. I flew to Cincinnati.

We were a little like Abbot and Costello—Frank, a seventy-year-old, old-school Italian Catholic dude, and me, a progressive Jewish guy twenty years his junior. We grow close very quickly.

In Cincinnati, we stayed at the Garfield Suites Hotel. We had dinner, and I was careful to get very hydrated and not drink alcohol. I went to bed early. The next day was the biggest in my business life so far.

I woke up early and went down to the dingy gym for a quick, intense workout. Naturally, I started the day with a healthy breakfast. I showered and got dressed. I was ready. I stood still, breathing in the moment. Tears ran down my face. We had a dream. We wanted to help Americans eat better to take a bite out of disease. We followed our dream. We fought, clawed, sacrificed, and worked hard to get there. We had the opportunity of a lifetime. Jennifer and I had a crazy idea in our kitchen. Yes, we were in fifty Whole Foods stores and fifty Wegmans. Now we were looking at four-digit numbers. We had a meeting with the most significant supermarket chain in North America.

The tears kept coming. No matter the outcome of this meeting, I thought, I accomplished something that I set my mind to, that I willed into happening. I knew my father would be proud of me.

Frank and I walked down the street and met with another broker, Larry Hood. We rode the elevator upstairs and entered the conference room to meet with a woman aptly named Michelle Kroger. She was the head dairy buyer for all Kroger supermarkets, a very powerful person. Frank poured the B'more Organic samples. I went through my canned sales pitch. Five minutes in, Michelle's assistant, Sharita, rushed in late. She downed a few samples during my spiel.

"And, they're all organic, made with no added sugar. We give 1 percent of sales to MS and breast cancer research—"

Sharita interrupted. "Mmmmm. Delicious. Oh my god, these are good. Can I try the mango one, please?"

"Um, sure," I responded, not sure if I should be angry to be interrupted or astonished at how much she loved the product.

Frank handed her more.

My pitch didn't last long. In fact, I didn't even get to finish it. After only a few minutes Michelle and Sharita were brainstorming about what regions the product would work in, what flavors to choose, and in how many of their 2,400 stores. I knew enough about sales and negotiations to shut up. It was the easiest sales call in my entire life.

We flew home.

I had another business trip a few days after Kroger. I came home late, and as always, I arose early. I poured a steaming hot cup of coffee from the machine that was set for 5:30 a.m. I checked my email, as was my compulsion. I also had a strange habit of checking my spam daily.

There it was in my spam folder: an email from Michelle Kroger having us fill out paperwork to be in all twelve of Kroger's regions: more than one thousand stores.We did it! Our silly idea was accepted to be on the shelves of Kroger.

The Mountaineering Entrepreneur

When it comes to dressing for meetings, I'm from the old school—business casual. Andrew showed up looking like the mountaineering entrepreneur that he is—jeans, a B'more Organic fleece vest, and a big backpack. He wanted to portray all his loves, and sure enough, Michelle Kroger liked what she saw and heard. We sold four items into 1,500 to 2,000 stores in most of their divisions across the U.S.

—Frank Rich

From then on, Frank and I were like a bowling team. He'd miraculously set up meetings at leading supermarket chains, and we'd bowl 'em over: Harris Teeter, Lowes Foods, and Publix. We were on fire.

Thanks to Frank, we got on the shelves in more than 2,500 stores and rode a wave of 270 percent annual compound sales growth. That's what earned us the fifth-place ranking on *Inc.* magazine's list of fastest growing natural/organic brands.

How fast we turned from pain to passion!

NOTHING FOCUSES
THE MIND LIKE FEAR

"The most difficult thing is the decision to
act. The rest is merely tenacity."

–Amelia Earhart

"Damn, it, Andy! Get your freaking ass down here. Right now!" mild-mannered Geo screamed at me.

I was on one of my first expeditions, and my first-time up Mount Whitney. The famous mountaineer, George "Geo" Dunn, guided us. Geo started as a guide on Mount Rainier in 1975. He held the record for summiting Mount Rainier—more than five hundred times. He participated in climbing expeditions the world over, including four expeditions to Everest, summiting in 1991, and the North Face of Kanchenjunga, the world's third-highest peak. He co-owns the expedition company International Mountain Guides.

Like most guides I know, Geo seems as if he has ice water in his veins. He's super nice, and approachable too, and like my friends Chris

Warner and Dan Jenkins, very laid back—until you got in trouble.

In case I haven't communicated it well enough by this point, I'm not a mountaineer. I'm a guy who likes to go mountaineering. I can barely tie a knot, I struggle to apply sunscreen, and I have been known to lose a crampon at inopportune times.

On the descent from camp two back to camp one on Mount Whitney, there was a steep, icy stretch that I didn't much care for. I was the slowest and last person to tackle it. Not having had much crampon experience in dicey, icy conditions, I traversed the mountain slowly to avoid going straight down like the others.

Clearly, I was taking too long for Geo. The next thing I knew, my cramponed boots pointed straight down the slope and managed to hold me securely. I down-climbed quickly and safely. Lesson learned.

A few years later, I relayed this story to Chris Warner from Earth Treks shortly after I met him.

"Oh yeah," Chris said. "That's an old guiding trick. Nothing focuses the mind like fear."

He was right.

I remembered that lesson on subsequent expeditions. One time on a technical section on Rainier we experienced a sensation on a knife ridge. The team climbed over rocks, hearing the scraping metal sounds as our spiked crampons hit them. On either side, I could see a thousand-foot drop. Clank. Then my foot slipped a little when a rock came loose. That kind of slip makes you pull whoever you're roped to, and you jerk again, causing you to wobble side to side, each time leaning toward one cliff and then the other.

We climbed for hours. Still, muscle fatigue evaporated. Thoughts of business problems and the fight with my wife before I left merged and became laser beams of focus. All my senses heightened as I continued to concentrate on the little problem right there. Concentrate. Use adrenaline, that fight-or-flight hormone surging through my body made to protect me from the lion about to eat me. Use it to make my muscles stronger and my endurance longer.

Focusing on Flat Ground

Fear will focus your mind on flat ground as well. It works on our expeditions through life. I used it in my business.

It was late December 2012, the time of the year when daylight is painfully scarce, when the damp cold on the East Coast seeps into your bones. It's time when some of us get seasonal affective disorder, also called SAD, a form of depression brought on by the lack of sunlight. Getting out of bed in the dark is hard on a good day. It's more challenging when you're running a startup whose cash is falling close to zero.

That morning it was nearly impossible to get out of bed. I had received the news the day before.

We had just cracked the New York City market. Our broker came through for us and landed a great distributor covering the bodegas. It was going to be big. We had been selling basically by the case. Those guys ordered by the pallet. It amounted to 180 cases a week. Once our product was successful in those small stores, the brokers were confident we could get placed in the New York offices of Bloomberg and Google. Those companies provide free snacks to their massive and hard-working office staff. They buy product by the pallet weekly.

Our big break.

We had made one delivery to them two months before. One customer called and told us the bottles were bloating before the expiration date. It was caused by too much yeast in the bottle. It wasn't dangerous, it just gave it a foul taste like OJ that's sort of turned. The customer was understanding, but I wasn't as understanding with our manufacturer, who was endangering our life savings. Of course, I let the company making our smoothie have it for that terrible mistake. I told the customer it wouldn't happen again.

Just before New Year's, we received the call that it happened again. The third and final time. It wasn't my fault directly. It was because of a mistake made by the manufacturer. Ultimately that's my responsibility.

Bye, New York City. Bye, hundreds of bodegas; bye, Google and Bloomberg. We lost a huge opportunity exactly at the time when we needed the cash. I wanted to just pull the warm covers over my head, bury myself in pillows, and avoid the cold, dark morning. Maybe avoid the day altogether. I worked in our house at the time, so no one would notice if I just stayed in bed for days.

If you've never experienced SAD or depression, it's like a deep fog rolls in and engulfs you, bringing fatigue and mental pain. I'd rather be on a short rope on a knife's edge than in that scary business situation. We had little to no cash, and we just lost a huge account. Clearly our co-packer was having major challenges that had to be fixed yesterday. It meant no income for my family. The reality was we'd lose the whole business in a few weeks, our health insurance, and our life savings with it. There was much I could do. It was easier to stay under the covers.

Fear. We were about to lose everything.

Nothing focuses the mind like fear.

Okay, tune out the distractions. Don't look at the cliffs on either side or worry about the bad things that can happen. Breathe. Concentrate on each step required to get off this ledge and onto safer ground.

Call Dr. Frank Lee and get him down to the plant this week to find out what's wrong.

Make a dozen calls to potential investors to get cash in right away.

Make another dozen sales calls every day.

Get out of bed. Focus; keep putting one foot in front of the other. You've been comfortable being uncomfortable. You'll get through this treacherous section.

We did.

THERE ARE NO STRAIGHT LINES TO A SUMMIT

"The credit belongs to the man who is actually in the arena, whose face is marred by dust and sweat and blood; who strives valiantly; who errs, who comes short again and again…and who at the worst, if he fails, at least fails while daring greatly."

—Theodore Roosevelt

I hoped the third time would be the charm.

I originally met Kathi Levine, who was on the first Jodi's Climb for Hope expedition, at a six-day mountaineering course on Mount Rainier in 2002. We honed our knot-tying, crevasse-rescuing, and ice-axing skills before attempting to summit with another classmate named Ari, but the bitter cold and unrelenting blizzard eliminated any possibility of climbing to the top.

The snow had also thwarted my first attempt on Mount Rainier the year before, so it was strike two for me.

Kathi, Ari, and I decided to have a reunion and try Mount Rainier again by ourselves, without a guide. Often guiding companies rush you up and down, which makes it hard with little rest and a grueling pace. It's not nearly as much fun to rush to the summit, and guides get paid whether you make it or not.

Ari was a member of a mountain rescue team and said his buddies would come out and join our expedition. That news was great. I was glad someone could help tie the knots and assist, God forbid, if we fell into a crevasse. I felt better about taking on the risky mountain without guides.

We received drip emails from Ari's buddies dropping out. The last guy to bail said something about never wanting to climb with that guy Ari. I called Kathi. She too was a little concerned. We discussed canceling the trip and then decided what the heck. We didn't have to summit if we didn't feel safe. It would be a great escape from the oppressive East Coast August weather.

We arrived in Washington State on August 4, 2002, and met up at Whitaker's Bunkhouse, an hour outside Mount Rainier Park. We started our climb on August 5. The section from the base, called Paradise, to Camp Muir was pretty straightforward. There weren't a lot of challenges, but it was a tough hike with a forty-five-pound pack. A shocking amount of the April snow was gone, making the trip a different experience. The bottom section was mostly a dirt trail, where in previous years the snow line started at Paradise. The snowless trek did take its toll on our feet, but without snow it was also hard to get lost.

Ari, who seemed to have packed on a few pounds in four months, was moving slowly. I'm no speed demon, yet I couldn't go slow enough to prevent from going too far ahead. Kathi and I wound up speaking to a nice group of guys in another climbing group. When Ari finally caught up with us at a rest break, he complained that he had been working too many hours to train properly. It wasn't the ideal time to tell us. He also complained of bad blisters.

Over the six-hour ascent, I grew concerned about Ari's fitness and the condition of his feet. If he was moving so slowly over the "easy" section, there was no way he'd be able to summit. We'd never make the summit before the turnaround time. While waiting for Ari, we chatted with some nice guys on the ascent who were on the same schedule.

We planned to reach Camp Muir that afternoon. We'd melt snow to make water, prepare dinner, and then sleep. The guided trips would get up a few hours later, head to the summit, and return all the way to Paradise. It was dubbed a "Death March." That method was anything but paradise. We planned to lay low the following morning to rest, pack, eat, and melt a lot of snow to hydrate us.

Kathi and I also devised a backup plan in the event Ari couldn't go to the summit. We asked our new friends if we could make the summit attempt with them. They said we could go with them, but not tie into the same rope. We agreed.

Sure enough, Ari's blisters were debilitatingly painful. I had to have a tough conversation with him saying that it wasn't safe for him or our team if he climbed. He's wasn't happy, but he was gracious enough to tie the knots for us and make other preparations for the climb. The group of guys told us to meet them at their tents at midnight, and we'd go with them.

We retired to our sleeping bags well before sunset.

"My brain knew this was a mistake."

I love Kathi. There, I said it. I love Kathi. She's a kind, generous, loving person and sharp entrepreneur. The Charlotte, North Carolina, native speaks with a slow southern drawl. And she moves in a slow southern way. My ADHD didn't always mesh with Kathi's southern ways. I set the alarm extra early. There was no way I was going to miss our escort from the guys at midnight. I left a full hour of prep time—getting dressed, eating, and readying our packs. Still, I found myself yelling at her, "Come on, Krazy Kathi, let's go! We're going to miss those guys." After fifty-nine belligerent minutes, we tied into Ari's knots and made our way to the guys' tents.

Their tents were dark and silent.

It was exactly midnight. There was no way we missed them.

"Guys? Guys? You in there?" I called out.

"Oh, shit! We overslept. Sorry," one of them answered.

Now what? We couldn't take a chance on when those guys were going to go, if at all.

Neither Kathi nor I were proficient at crevasse rescue, and there were only two of us on the rope. Three is a much safer number. Neither of us knew the route. We were missing a few other crucial skills as well.

It was a crazy beautiful night. The combination of the moonlight and snow provided ideal visibility. I could see far into the distance. The temperature was perfect. It wasn't freezing like on my other climbs. I felt a slight, warm breeze. It was hard to believe it was the same mountain and same spot that dumped three feet of snow in five days on us just four months earlier.

We had traveled all this way. We had trained. It was my third attempt. We were dressed and ready to go, tied in.

Still, my brain knew it was a mistake to try it with only Kathi. We weren't fully prepared for the section. I always said I'd avoid making dumb decisions on the mountain. I'd live to climb again. The mountain would be there. I did a gut check: going with only two of us didn't make sense.

I looked at Kathi behind me to get a sense of what we should do. She shrugged, knowing the best decision was not the one we wanted. She didn't want to make the call either.

I said, "Okay, up we go." With that, we headed toward the Cathedral Gap on our way to the summit.

Fortunately, the rangers had placed three-foot-high wooden sticks in the snow. The sticks had small, bright orange flags on them to provide better route visibility during bad weather. Those plus a well-worn path and the moonlight made route-finding easy. We even saw other climbers' headlamps in the distance showing us the way. My anxiety melted away with each step toward our goal.

After forty-five minutes of pure joy on that gorgeous night, we arrived at the rocky base of the Gap, a steep section leading us to the Ingraham Flats, where there were no flags, no well-worn snow path, and no headlamps in sight.

There was a very faint trail in the dusty section. There were also bits of snow that had come off people's boots, meaning others had recently been there. We followed those signs until they too disappeared.

We walked slowly over the rocky incline, making our way up with crampons on the rocks. It was a little challenging. I stopped to catch my breath, tried to find the route, and prayed we were heading in the right direction. I looked up, and there were our buddies who had overslept. We weren't lost. We followed them before they left us in the dust.

We kept heading up in the direction of the group. After thirty minutes we reached the top of Disappointment Cleaver. A snow path was so evident that Kathi and I could follow the route to the summit. The sun was rising, along with our confidence. Until Kathi's fatigue set in. She began to stop every few minutes. I knew from the seminar and previous Rainier expeditions that we had to be regimented. We had to climb nonstop for an hour before earning a break. Kathi thought we earned a break every five minutes. At that rate we'd never make the summit before our turnaround time. The snow bridges over the crevasse would melt. I didn't feel like pulling Krazy Kathi out of a crevasse, and I doubted Kathi would remember how to pull me out.

I turned and shouted backward into the wind. "Come on, Kath! Let's go. We have to keep moving. We can't keep stopping."

In her slow southern accent, Kathi answered, "I'm tired. I need a break."

Climbers are supposed to keep slack in the rope in case someone falls. It allows climbers time to self-arrest in the snow, preventing the team from sliding into danger below—a rock outcropping or a crevasse. Instead, I used the rope to pull her up the mountain, not the soundest decision I've ever made. We had to move faster. We argued like an old married couple for hours while I tried to pick up the pace and reach the summit in time.

We climbed up a big step and had a better view. Once on top of that ledge, we saw familiar faces, our late-sleeping friends. We arrived at the volcano caldera at almost the same time. From there it was a relatively easy thirty-minute hike with only a slight incline to the true summit above the crater.

We did it! Kathi and I climbed to the summit of Mount Rainier. She was fairly spent but still overjoyed with our accomplishment. We hugged and celebrated and took photos. Kathi wanted to keep celebrating and keep taking photos. It was gorgeous, a Mount Rainier Chamber of Commerce kind of day, and it was likely a once-in-a-lifetime event, but falling through a snow bridge could be an end-of-life event. I used some not nice words to tell Kathi I wasn't going to pull her out of a crevasse.

We fought again before I could convince her to leave. I felt better because the other group of guys was leaving too. It was a good sign that we weren't too late. We followed them off the summit ridge, turned left, and made the steep, steep descent. Kathi was in the lead on our rope and we quickly fell behind the other group again.

After about thirty minutes the lead climber in the group ahead of us stopped way down the slope. He waved his arms and yelled. We were too far away to hear what he was saying. He seemed frantic, so we hustled down to see what the heck was going on.

When we approached we could finally make out what he was screaming. "Stop! Stop! We're going the wrong way."

Are you kidding me? We just descended for more than a half-hour down a huge face. We would have to climb back up for an hour to get back to where we started. No! The word *disheartening* doesn't come close to describing the despair of having to race back up the mountain unnecessarily before our butts fell into oblivion. We managed to keep moving, albeit slowly, back up the terrain we had just descended. The combination of fatigue, sadness, and the fact that those other guys got us into that mess made Kathi and me a team again. We labored ourselves back to the summit ridge and down the *correct* way this time.

We had to hustle. We made great progress back down. Neither of us had any major issues other than exhaustion and extreme dehydration. We were alive, heading in the right direction. It was all downhill from there. A stream of people was heading down, and we kept pace with them.

After sixteen hours we made it back to Camp Muir. Tired. Safe. Alive. I crawled into my bag and took a huge nap.

From then on, for any highly technical climbs, I always chose to hire a guide.

"We can make anything happen."

Over the many Jodi's Climb for Hope expeditions, Jennifer and I developed a close relationship with Ricky Haro, our guide from Rare Earth Adventures. Ricky became Jennifer's trusted friend. Not only did he build a great guiding company, but he is also a good man, always willing to go the extra mile for us. He never made money on our trips, and I think he even lost money on each one.

In 2016 I showed Ricky a video of a twelve-year-old girl with transverse myelitis (TM), a disease similar to MS. With MS it's a combination of many lesions that contribute to impairment over time. With TM, a person suddenly gets one massive lesion on the spine. The TM victim is immediately and permanently paralyzed. I talked to

Ricky about the young TM patient's wish to climb a mountain. "Hey, what do you think?" I asked Ricky. "Can we do this? Can we make it happen?"

"Yeah, we can make anything happen," Ricky said.

The Brotherhood of a Rope

Andy and I have developed a friendship that goes beyond the mountains. I call it the "brotherhood of a rope." On a mountain, a rope keeps a group of people together who have to rely on each other.

Andy and I have relied on each other for the last fourteen years, and he has helped me in many ways. As owners of growing businesses with little room for error, we've faced similar challenges and spoken often on the phone to help each other. We would have never reached our current level of trust and comfort with each other had we not shared experiences on the mountain together. His willingness to be open and transparent about what happened with his business and how he overcame the challenges was a key to the success of my business.

—Ricky Haro
Managing Member
Rare Earth Adventures

How to get that twelve-year-old girl up a mountain was an unknown. Guides are trained in high-angle rescue and in lowering people, but pulling somebody up a mountain was a different story. The logistics of the trip for the girl never worked out, but the idea of pulling some-body who can't walk up a mountain resonated with me. Why not take Jen up Mount Adams?

Jen, who normally doesn't back down from challenges, was hesitant. She never saw herself as handicapped at all or needing special help for doing anything. If Jen was going to participate in an activity, she would be an active participant like everyone else.

Jill Green, Danny Kaplan's wife, was always great about letting Danny climb with Tiger and me every year, but this time she had a different idea. "MS and breast cancer adversely affect women. It's my turn to climb with you," Jill said.

Hard to argue with that logic. Women started signing up. The trip quickly filled up, mostly with Jill's friends. Finally and reluctantly, Jennifer decided to go for it.

We all arrived in Portland and went to the Rare Earth office. There it was: a tricked-out wheelchair. It had mountain bike tires that popped off and could be replaced with skis for when we hit the snow line. It was affixed to a metal bar so it could be used as a chariot to steer around obstacles. On that bar were places for other climbers to tie in and pull it like a dog sled. Rare Earth Adventures recruited a lot of vol-unteers and paid guides for the expedition. We needed female guides for the all-women's team and volunteers to pull Jen's wheelchair up the mountain. The latter was made up of former military dudes and professional guides. And me.

We assembled the mountain chair while the women's team departed first. Our group left a bit later, pulling Jennifer through the relatively flat section, meandering through the pine forest. You never realize how rocky a trail is until you constantly have to weave around the

"The muscle guys" pulled Jen up Mount Adams

large rocks so the wheels won't get stuck, watching your wife's head swaying like a bobblehead toy. My gut hurt watching it. I had no idea how Jen was going to make the arduous climb. I was the steering guy who pushed the handle to get the mountain chair moving in the right direction and navigating the rocks. The muscle guys did most of the pulling. I assumed it was going to be easy for her sitting in a chair, but her body took a pounding.

As the incline and altitude increased, our "sled dogs" got a little winded. We took more frequent breaks than I expected. Ricky is a former Air Force survival instructor. His job was to help get personnel out from behind enemy lines. The guy doesn't get rattled. I conversely panicked about the pace and the pounding Jen's body was taking, especially the many times she had to get out of the chair and hike for hundreds of yards up steep boulder fields, all at relatively high altitude.

Thank goodness for Ashley Worden. An amazing woman, friend, and nurse. She had climbed Cotopaxi, Kili, and Adams with us before. She and her husband, Ben, raised a lot of money for Jodi's Climb for Hope.

Presidents have a person to handle all their stuff. They're a special assistant, an aid commonly called a "body man." We recruited Ashley to be Jen's body person. Ashley jumped at the chance to help. Her job was to shadow Jen everywhere. She managed Jen's meds and monitored her for medical issues. She also played middle person to Ricky and me. Ricky wanted Jen to walk up a huge boulder field. I lost my composure and demanded his military buddies carry her. Ashley just said, "Okay, Jen, here we go," and walked her slowly up the field.

We finally reached the snowfield. We thought it was going to be easier. It was much harder.

The challenge went on for hours. I previously had no clue how hard it was going to be for Jennifer—the walking, the jostling, keeping her core upright when the sled tilted. The heat, the cold. It was brutal, and as challenging for her as it was for us. Perhaps the biggest challenge was trusting Ricky and the team. Her life was in his hands.

After eight hours we finally approached The Lunch Counter, where we would set up camp. We heard screaming and hollering from the all-women's team rooting us on. I cried. It wasn't the summit, but it was still a major accomplishment. I'd been there more than six times. It was a dream to show Jen those breathtaking vistas the spot affords a weary climber.

After everyone quickly looked down at Mount Saint Helens and Mount Hood, the group got Jen into the tent and her warm sleeping bag. Hot drinks and dinner quickly followed. She was out for the night.

We had an early five a.m. wake-up call to get a jump on the mountain. It took a while to get out of camp with all the other climbers up there. We were an hour behind schedule. We managed to get out ahead of the women's team.

From that point, it was all snow up to the summit. And steep. The pulling team was a bit spent from the huge effort the prior day. We moved slowly, compounded with snow building up under the skis that we didn't expect. As we got higher, we moved even slower.

The all-women's group had one team of really fast-moving climbers. They volunteered to also pull the sled, possibly giving up their summit attempt.

The last five hundred vertical feet were brutal before Piker's Peak at 11,500 feet. A normal climbing rate is one thousand vertical feet an hour. It took us two hours. As we approached the extremely steep last twenty-five feet, I was the lead dog, and I got a surge of adrenaline. I screamed at the team to pull harder to reach that milestone. I reached flat ground first and started running. Jen's sled was still on the thirty-degree incline, and the increased speed jerked the sled, causing it to tilt deeply. Jen thought it would be best to bail out. She did, and she started sliding down the steep mountain. Ashely, who was shadowing Jen, was the last thing standing between Jen and a one-thousand-foot slide. As she was trained, Ashley dove on top of Jen and used her ice axe to self-arrest the duo—textbook snow-school mountaineering skills.

Jen walked the last ten feet. There Ricky huddled with the guides and pulled me into the conversation.

Ricky recalled the moment we made it to Piker's Peak, aka The False Summit, at 11,200 feet.

> We battled it out all the way up within about a thousand feet of the summit, and I think at that point everybody realized that the summit was still a really far, far-reaching goal. Jen had her close friends with her—an all-female team that was climbing together. We had a huge crew of guys pulling her up, and it was tough to concede that we might have gotten her as high as we could, but we were running out of time and had to stop and turn around. It was heartbreaking.

We released the female volunteers to go on without us. They were in tears like everyone else. We handed them our flag, which reached the summit with them.

"I'm coming back to do Adams."

Ten months later, in the summer of 2017, Jen started having some major difficulties. She had even greater pain and weakness in her left arm. Jen knows herself well. She got scared and quiet about it. She finally spoke up, and we raced to see Dr. Calabresi. He ordered MRIs, and we met with him shortly afterward.

Indeed, Jen had another significant lesion on her spine corresponding to where she was having the issues with her left arm. After five-plus years with no new lesions, she got a big one. That meant her current medication wasn't working and the disease was marching again, attacking her spinal cord. She couldn't afford more of those lesions.

She cried and cried and tucked herself away. Two days later she emerged. Her first call was to Ricky. "I'm coming back to do Adams again in a month. If this disease is going to take me down, there are things I need to do beforehand. Summiting Mount Adams is one of them. Can you do it?"

Ricky answered, "Can we do it in a month? We've been waiting for this call. We're ready, and we have a much better plan for this attempt." This is how he remembers Jen's Summit Attempt 2.0:

Jen and Andy on Mount Adams.
On a summit again together.

Jen committed to getting herself physically ready and able to help us where we needed help, and all of us had a higher level of commitment to get to the top.

Jen was an inspiration to watch. When she flew into Portland for the climb she was barely moving, but looking back I think she was being purposeful in all her movements to conserve energy. On Mount Adams, she got up and walked at certain times—a hundred yards across a rock field at one point—where the year before, we had to carry her. Those walks of hers threw Andy for a loop because he was concerned about her strength, but she was focused and knew she had to walk some on her own to make it all the way.

The scene as we approached the summit was one of the most surreal I've ever witnessed on a mountain. That year a throng of butterflies had stormed the entire Pacific Northwest, and when we were fifty yards from the summit, out of nowhere thousands and thousands of purple butterflies swarmed down on us. Jen got out of the sled and took off running to the summit. Andy ran after her, freaking out and yelling at her to stop. She made it to the top and jumped up and down, butterflies flying all around her and landing on her. Soon Andy and a couple of other people who were on the climb joined Jen and the butterflies in the celebration. It was totally one of the best summit experiences that I've ever observed.

Ricky's new strategic plan worked. He helped our dream of standing on a summit together come true.

Jen, ever the stubborn wife, insisted on walking the last half mile alone. She wanted to enjoy the serenity and take in the beauty. Before departing she had made me sit in the chair in the relatively flat section.

I laughed and obliged. Wow! What a scary experience, giving control to someone else as I bounced and sped down a slight decline. I had seen how great the challenge was for Jen. Sitting in that chair for ten minutes greatly enhanced my appreciation for her effort.

A lot of credit was heaped upon the people pulling the chair. The experience of being in the chair was transformational for me. Jen transformed as well. She learned to trust others, to stop trying to control things she couldn't. And she learned just how strong she really was.

"It's how we respond that's important."

As one of my business coaches, Don Schminche, used to say, "The next time things go as planned, it will be the first time. No plan survives its collision with reality." To put it another way, "Man plans and God laughs." This is true in all our businesses and our lives. We have a dream or plan that we pursue. There are always unforeseen challenges—deaths, personal illness, lost employment, or simple reality. Of course, it's how we respond to the challenges that's important. I watched Jen respond to her bad news.

At age fifty-five, I'm not living the life I planned at twenty-five, but I am living the life I was given. It is funny what the universe gives us sometimes. My mother died when I was a baby, leaving me with no memories of her and being adopted young. That situation seems hard, yet I'm now raising two children who don't even know their mother's name. When I try to comfort my kids, they say, "Yeah, Dadda, but at least you know who she was and knew your father."

The route to a summit is never a straight line and isn't always as we see it on the map. In all my business leadership positions, we did the same thing we did in the mountains: came back from our

There are no straight lines to the summit on Mount Rainier

setbacks; huddled; got feedback from the team, mentors, and experts in the field; and tried it a different way. We met with our climbing team, consulted the park rangers, and found a safe way to the summit around any gnarly serac.

Our original plan for B'more Organic was to make cups of skyr. Reality dictated that we make a drinkable product, so we went at it another way. The shift didn't change our mission or vision. It allowed us to accomplish what we set out to do.

After my mother and father died young and my sister Jodi and wife Jennifer got sick, my mission in life came to me: to take a bite out of disease. Most people die without ever knowing their life's purpose.

Jennifer and I started Jodi's Climb for Hope. The universe associated my father and me with women and disease. First my mother, and then my grandmother died when I was seven. My sister died when I was forty-four. And Jennifer was diagnosed with MS five months into our marriage.

We knew little about cancer research, so we reached out to experts at Johns Hopkins to educate us. Our progress was too slow. Jodi died, and we reassessed our situation. I studied what was going on in the cancer community and met with experts who knew far more than me. That's when we decided to start a for-profit entity to make healthier food options and donate money to research to make it easier to get to the summit.

We knew nothing about the food industry—heck, we couldn't even make yogurt in our kitchen. I called one of the leading, most successful people in the beverage industry. The same way I was close to Johns Hopkins, I was close to Seth Goldman, at that time the CEO and co-founder of Honest Tea, based in Maryland. He readily agreed to give me free advice. He said that if our thing was "No Added Sugar," that information needed to be more prominent on our labels. We changed our labels. When his book *Message in a Bottle* came out, Jennifer and I treated it as one-part road map for our business and one-part book club, where we dissected each page and discussed and debated how it applied to B'more Organic.

Our sales-growth graph looked like a hockey stick, and then Chobani and other brands started producing competitive products in smaller bottles at lower prices, and the pricing disparity became a competitive problem. But when you're already on the shelf, making even a slight change is difficult, and making a dramatic change from sixteen ounces to 12.8 ounces destroys your pricing structure. Kroger took our price-per-bottle down, but Publix didn't follow suit, and sales declined.

We found a new manufacturing facility where we could make even more profit, but after a year of delays and only one production run in 2019, the manufacturer illegally terminated our contract. We had nowhere to make our smoothies. It would take five months to change the bottles and labels over to a new copacker. We couldn't carry our employees for five months, and neither could we keep our coveted shelf space at premier retailers such as Whole Foods and Kroger. We didn't have five months of cash reserves to cover rent and insurance with no sales.

After playing three-dimensional chess for more than eight years, we faced checkmate. We couldn't move. We had always found ways to overcome challenges, to fulfill our mission. Even Sarah Frisch, our operations manager who knew the gravity of the situation, was optimistic: "I know you'll pull this out like you've done dozens of other times."

I tried, but I was on a mountain, low on sustenance, unable to make food or melt snow for water, and overlooking a dark crevasse. Our money was gone. Our dream was gone, our route to the summit blocked. It was like the time Tiger, Alissa, Danny, Kelly, and I were on Rainier. The fifty-mile-an-hour winds kicked up. We went to sleep early waiting for our one a.m. wake-up call from the guides. Instead, some stranger rapped on our tents at eleven p.m., telling us the ladder over the large crevasse near the summit had fallen in. There was no safe way to the summit. Our route was blocked. It was time to head back down and attack the mountain another time and another way.

The same was true for B'more Organic. There was no safe way forward. Once we went out of production for five months, we'd lose our coveted shelf space at Whole Foods and Kroger. It was too dangerous to keep spending money if we didn't know we could keep going.

People ask me why people are so dumb that they die on Everest. Turning around and going home is much harder than people realize. To climb Everest you pay $65,000, spend months training, and put your life on hold for more than three months. It takes that long to travel there, trek to basecamp, and then climb the mountain. If there's an issue on the mountain you have to make the decision whether to turn back or not. Going through your mind—which is already not thinking clearly from the limited oxygen—you're thinking "I just spent $65,0000 and three months of my life. I have only one shot at this. I can't turn around this close to my goal."

That's when people die.

Andy envisioned a product and built it into a successful venture. He got shelf space in hundreds of stores across the United States of America. He did everything right except selling the company for a bazillion dollars.

—Eric Kronthal

Fortunately, I'm comfortable being uncomfortable. I'm back at it on another route. I've learned not to say, "Shoot, that other route is better, easier, or more scenic." You can't control the weather or mountain conditions. You say, "This is the safest and most viable route the mountain is giving me today." Take it. Take it; get to the summit; reach your goal and get home to your family.

My lows certainly have been lower and more frequent than many other people's. The highs have been higher as well, giving me the best views of this wonderful time on earth.

The gravity pulling me to my bed returned after B'more Organic closed. The "It's how we respond" phrase also returned, along with the need to feed my family. I instinctively kept putting one foot in front of the other, taking one step at a time. I had to work doing anything I could for income.

With the publishing of this book, I became an author. If I can do it, anyone can. I had always given motivational keynote speeches, and after one where I received particularly strong reviews, I decided to go pro. I invested a lot of time and money getting set up to give motivational speeches, encouraging people never to give up, keep putting one foot in front of the other, because they have flags to carry. The effort resulted in a bunch of paid gigs right away.

The COVID-19 pandemic then hit and everything came to a screeching halt. No one was hosting events or paying speakers.

At just that time, my friend Ricky Haro, who's earning his Ph.D. in instructional design and taking his career in a new direction, approached me with an offer to donate Rare Earth Adventures to Jodi's Climb for Hope. Combining the entities would increase our fundraising capacity and the amount we can donate to cancer and MS research. My new role as director of a first-class guiding company also gives me an alternate route to fulfilling my lifelong mission and vision. Growing Rare Earth Adventures means more people will be outside and moving, which, like natural foods, is a great way to help people "b'more" healthy. Being outside and taking people to see sunsets over Mount Hood is a gift. I'm loving this new route through life until something inevitably pops up to force me to go another way to my goal.

"Tell me, what is it you plan to do
with your one wild and precious life?"

—Mary Oliver

ABOUT THE AUTHOR

Andrew Buerger is an award-winning entrepreneur of for-profit and nonprofit organizations. He is the founder of Jodi's Climb for Hope, which has raised $850,000 for MS and breast cancer research by getting more than two hundred fifty climbers safely to the summits on four continents. He is also the director of Rare Earth Adventures, an expedition guiding company based in Portland, Oregon.

Andy lives in Baltimore with his loving wife, Jennifer, and two children. They recently added a new dog into their family named Denali.

CPSIA information can be obtained
at www.ICGtesting.com
Printed in the USA
BVHW020623211221
624562BV00004B/31